# Move
# Your Own Way
## 10th Anniversary Edition

This little black book that contains…
The Secret Psychology of Success

Written by Cherry A. Collier, Ph.D.

Edited by Nicole D. Collier

# DEDICATION

I dedicate this book to my champion, my cheerleader, the one who carried me in her womb (and bears the scars on her womb – and she never complained).

Mom, I wrote this for you so that you will always know what resources you have inside of you!  You are the wind beneath my wings.  God will continue to lift you up and answer your prayers.  God certainly hears you – that is why I was sent here!  I love you for all you are and all you have given me!   You are rich beyond measure with all the beauty you have inside of you.

I love you!

*Mini Me*

**The Fruits of Learning Publishing**

For additional information please visit us on the web at
www.drcherrycoaching.com

Email us at askdrcherry@gmail.com

# ACKNOWLEDGEMENTS

I acknowledge that nothing on this earth happens without support from others and God!

Thank you to my wonderful parents for ALWAYS believing in me. I wish the world could experience the love and support that I get from you both every day. If it did, there would be no drug use or ignorance because everyone would find a way to make you proud of them. Even if it took all they had! That is how great you both are!

Dad, thanks for always letting me know that I can and for celebrating my EVERY accomplishment!

Thanks to my family, my sistah girls, and friends for your unwavering support! I love you and I am blessed to have a village beside and backing me! I acknowledge each person in the village that has contributed to me in anyway!

Nicole Collier, you are a truly beautiful being. I am so grateful to have you as my cousin, my editor and my friend. The universe sent you straight to me with your wisdom and knowledge. Without you, this book would still be a dream! Thanks for sharing in the vision! I appreciate your long hours and unselfish help. I acknowledge your mom – though she isn't on the earth, she is here in spirit and supports you daily.

Betsy Walraven, you are an Angel on earth. Thank you for always asking how you can help and then helping!

You are a treasure!  Thanks for bringing your brother (Joe) along to help too.  You guys are simply the best!

Thanks Pearly "Satvinder" Dhingra and Erica Chapin for sitting in my office once a week for an entire semester mind mapping the project and encouraging me.

Thanks Marcia, Faye, Cameron, Butch, Alysia, Anita, Kim Roseberry and all my KSU students for being in my focus groups.

Thanks Greg Street for telling me to write a book for 3 years.  I listened.

Thanks Jonathan Sprinkles, Aqiyl Thomas and Del McNeal for your expertise and for sending me to the right places.

Thanks to Tad James and my Advanced Neuro Dynamics Family for your help with the content and expanding my awareness with your NLP courses.

Thanks Vincent McCant (www.atlantahapps.com) for being there for me.

Thanks to Dr. Wayne Dyer for being on PBS and expanding my view.

Thanks to my "shero" Oprah Winfrey. By making the Forbes list, you took away any excuse that I could ever have for not succeeding!

Thanks Sarah, Candace, Beege, Tom Tom, Tre', Justin, Baby Zo, Kayla, Brittany, and Brad, for giving me hope in the future. I took the path less traveled so that you can have a clearer path.

Tonjua, I wrote this book for you so that you will MOVE and be the powerful woman that you are!

To all of the great minds out there that allowed me to listen to your stories, read your books, watch your videos, learn from your workshops and feel from your soul – thanks! I have learned so much from the great writers of the past. I am only an instrument that is being used.


Namaste

# PREFACE

This book was created for you to manifest the power that is within you, now. I know that you already have what you need to be successful. Twelve simple lessons were developed to empower you with the tools, strategies and solutions to live a more fulfilled and abundant life. Each lesson is followed by an exercise that helps you integrate the learning immediately! You will put the lesson into action as soon as you read it. Over time, many sources of information have changed my perspective and paradigm; I included a few of these stories after each lesson, with hopes that they will inspire you even more. If you don't want to acquire the secrets to *MOVE Out of Your Own Way* – you must stop reading, now!

# TABLE OF CONTENTS

# INTRODUCTION
## The Most Powerful Drug

From the beginning of time, man (woman) has had the secret to healing any ailment, solving any problem, and making situations change. This secret, the most powerful drug there is, can cure ADD, depression, cancer, and the list goes on and on. The drug is called a placebo. A placebo is nothing more than your mind and your powerful mind can cure anything. In his book *Quantum Healing*, Deepak Chopra chronicles the fascinating mind-body connection and healing.

Others have written about this powerful drug as well. The January 20, 2003 edition of Time Magazine featured an article that highlighted the powerful weapon of the mind. As I read the article, it became apparent to me that in order for each of us to move out of our own way, we have to realize the power that exists **within** us. To begin to understand how to use this drug is to adopt the belief that this drug actually does exist. You see, it's pretty easy for us to think ideas like "What goes up must come down" or "The apple never falls far from the tree." It's easy for us to think these things because they've been around so long and they've become ingrained in our minds. We have internalized these ideas and incorporated them into our own personal belief system. We accept statements in our belief system as unconditionally true. We then use those truths to guide our decisions and our behaviors.

What has happened for many of us is we've created a belief system around things that in many cases actually aren't true such as, "Beauty is only skin deep" or "First impressions are last impressions." I'm reminded of the lyrics of an old song: "What a fool believes, he sees. The wise man has the power." Because we are wise people, we do have the power. With that power, I would like to suggest that you create an empowering belief system that constantly supports you. I suggest you create a belief system that keeps you on the cause side of equation.

Throughout our journey together, I'd like to introduce you to twelve empowering lessons that can help you cultivate the fruits within your life. If you adopt them, they will change your life forever. There are many more than twelve, but I believe these will lay the foundation for you to be empowered and in control of your life. In addition to the foundational lessons, you will find stories, poems, proverbs, and quotes that have moved or inspired me in some way. I have included them because I feel they truly resonate with the lessons in a practical, and easy to relate to way.

Once you understand the foundational concepts, I encourage you to add a few more of your own. What we want to do is create statements that are powerful beyond measure. We want to create a belief system that puts you in the driver's seat and leaves you there. Don't ever, I repeat, **don't ever** be a victim. Be in control of your communication, your mind, body and spirit.

Use that powerful drug, your mind, and be on the cause side of the equation.

"Our deepest fear is not that we are inadequate. Our deepest fear is that we are powerful beyond measure. It is our light, not our darkness that most frightens us. We ask ourselves, "Who am I to be brilliant, gorgeous, talented, and fabulous? Actually who are you not to be?

You are a part of this universe. Your playing small does not serve the world. There is nothing enlightened about shrinking so that other people won't feel insecure around you. We were born to manifest the glory that is within us. And as we let our light shine we unconsciously give other people permission to do the same. As we are liberated from our own fear, our presence automatically liberates others."

*Our Deepest Fear*
By: Marianne Williamson

# -1-
# Following the Yellow Brick Road to Success

I want to share a story with you. The main character is Dorothy. This is not an original story of mine... many of you have probably heard the story, or seen the movie *The Wiz* or *The Wizard of Oz*. Every time I see one of these movies, I see how we're all connected to Dorothy's story. What I'm going to share with you now is my version of Dorothy's trip down the yellow brick road to see the Wizard of Oz.

**Dorothy's Journey**
The story starts in Kansas. Dorothy realizes that things are no longer happening the way Dorothy wants them to happen. Her aunt and the other people around her are causing her stress. Someone is complaining about Toto and Dorothy is just in a slump.

Consider some parallels that you might have in your life. The bottom line is Dorothy is having a difficult day. Dorothy's having one of those days when you might want to say "Calgon! Take me away!" She begins to say things like, "I wish things were different," or "I wish I weren't here" (Have you ever said something like that before?). As the day continues, a storm starts to brew. As the storm starts to brew, things start to move. When you feel your life is in a bad place and things continue a downward spiral from bad to worse, this is the storm.

When the storm hits, Dorothy finds herself in unfamiliar territory. Dorothy puts herself in a hypnotic state, if you will, to deal with her unfamiliar surroundings. Now, in this new place, she's starting to manifest different things in her life; for instance, she starts to meet new people. It looks as though these people are looking at Dorothy with admiration instead of complaint (the grass looks greener).

Once she realizes she is no longer in Kansas (which while stressful, was familiar and comfortable), she starts to ask people to help her get home. She meets a witch who points her to Oz. Dorothy then envisions meeting the Wizard of Oz, who will immediately solve all of her problems. She fervently believes this individual is the key. Dorothy believes that this wizard, Oz, has the power to make her complete and to help her get home again. Unbeknownst to her, he is a mere mortal just like her.

### Seeking the Wizard

How many times in life have you believed that someone else had the power to complete you? That there is a so called Wizard of Oz out there to complete you? We're talking about a mortal "Wizard of Oz," let's be clear about this. I'm not speaking about God and the awesome power of God, because I certainly know that God is out there and was with Dorothy. However, knowing that God was with her, Dorothy was still looking for a man or a mortal person to help her, to make her complete. Have you ever put complete trust and faith in someone else to make you whole? How many times have we looked outside of us for those valuable gems, those powerful things that are actually already inside of us? They're inside of you now!

## Light-hearted in Hard Times

As Dorothy continues to ease on down the yellow brick road, she starts to sing a song that is even more telling of the situation at hand and helps to explain why this story is so important for us. From *The Wiz*: "Don't you carry nothing that might be a load/come on now/ease on down/ease on down the road." So, even in the song that she's singing, she's saying don't bring your baggage on this trip because we don't need the excessive weight to bring us down. All we need to do is to get to the wizard, because once we get to the wizard, everything is going to be okay! Another testament to our strength as humans is that in the midst of all of the turmoil that existed in her life, she had the fortitude to still sing. She had the ability to put the things out of her mind that were causing her frustration and to skip on down the road.

I know you see parallels to your incredible strength and tenacity because at times, you too are able to sing when you are hurting. Isn't it amazing, that as you look at everything in your life today you can still smile and sing? You can still have a good day, or as the old hymn says, "I've had some good days, I've had some bad days but overall I can't complain." Isn't it wonderful, just like Dorothy, we can ease on down that road and not let our baggage keep us back.

**Helping others find the power within**

On her journey to the wizard, Dorothy met a few people, the first of whom was called the Scarecrow. She actually met the Scarecrow in a cornfield. He tells Dorothy he is lost and he needs assistance because he doesn't have a brain. Dorothy helps him use the power within to heal himself – to use the brain he didn't realize he had. Dorothy was able to help the Scarecrow use the resources he had available to him to accomplish tasks. And you have resources available to you, don't you? After she assisted him, she invited him to join her as she journeyed to the wizard of Oz.

She then met the Tin Man who was stuck with no options and no hope of freedom. Dorothy used the magic inside of the Tin Man to help him realize he had a heart, which he thought he didn't have.

So far, the Scarecrow and the Tin Man, already had the resources they needed to be successful. You have those same resources that you need to be successful as well. Moving out of your own way is not about creating yourself. You came to this earth perfect and you came to this earth when you were called. Moving out of your own way allows you to appreciate what you already have inside of you so that you can be even more successful than you already are.

**Easing Farther Down the Road**

Dorothy meets another character named the Lion who lacked courage. The truth of the matter is, the Lion didn't lack courage. He simply lacked the knowledge that he had courage. You see, you have different strengths within yourself right now that you are not aware of. Because you are not aware of them, you may feel as if you don't have them. You do have them though. You just need to cultivate them.

So Dorothy was able to help the Lion realize that he had courage. Together, all of them went down the yellow brick road of life.

This book, *Move Out of Your Own Way,* is like the path that Dorothy took on that yellow brick road. We're going to go easily and effortlessly down the yellow brick road – life – and as we go down the road, we will meet and examine different characters or different people. Some of them might represent different parts of you. What we will realize is that each part of you already has what it needs to be successful. The only wizard you need to visit is the one in you.

**So Close, Yet Still So Far**
Eventually, they arrived to the wizard's castle. Once they got there, they realized that they had to go through obstacles and even more challenges to get a meeting with the wizard. Each time an obstacle was placed in front of them, Dorothy, the Scarecrow, the Tin Man and the Lion succeeded. They so believed in the power of this wizard, they refused to be defeated in their quest to meet him.

So they finally got to meet the Wizard and they found that the Wizard was really not a *wizard* at all. The Wizard was just a man. *Just a man.* That man didn't have any more power than what they had inside of themselves all along. The Wizard told Dorothy if she really wanted to go home, all she needed to do was click her heels.

Now get this, if you want to get home, if you want to discover a more abundant, more prosperous, healthier, and more productive life for yourself, all you have to do is click your heels. In other words, tap into your own resources. That's all you have to do. We are perfect as we are. We may not be flawless, but we are perfect. You were not born from lack; you came here perfect, on time, and right when you were supposed to be here. You are your greatest resource. All you need to do today, now, is realize that. Empower that greatness inside of you.

Click your heels, tap into your abundance, cultivate your fruits and be successful!

### A Lesson from a Sculptor
After Michelangelo completed the statue of David, he was asked how he could have made something so magnificent. Michelangelo replied, "The statue of David was already there, all I did was chip away."

Ladies and gentlemen, I submit to you that your greatness, your power, your magnificence is already available to you today, right now. All you have to do is chip away and uncover it.

# Yellow Brick Road

**What character in the Wiz story is most like you and why?**

_____
_____
_____
_____
_____
_____
_____
_____

**What would you like at the end of your "Yellow Brick Road?**

_____
_____
_____
_____
_____
_____
_____
_____

**What resources do you have inside of you that you are not using right now?**

_____
_____
_____
_____
_____
_____

Following the Yellow Brick Road to Success

## **Today I Delete**
## **Author Unknown**

Today I will delete from my diary two days:
yesterday and tomorrow

Yesterday was to learn
and tomorrow will be the consequence
of what I can do today.

Today I will face life
with the conviction that this day
will not ever return.

Today is the last opportunity
I have to live intensely,
as no one can assure me
that I will see tomorrow's sunrise.

Today I will be brave enough
not to let any opportunity pass me by,
my only alternative is to succeed.

Today I will invest
my most valuable resource:
my time,
in the most transcendental work:
my life;

I will spend each minute
passionately to make

of today a different
and unique day in my life.

Today I will defy every obstacle
that appears on my way trusting
I will succeed.

Today I will resist
pessimism and will conquer
the world with a smile,
with the positive attitude
of always expecting the best.

Today I will make of every ordinary task
a sublime expression.

Today I will have my feet on the ground
understanding reality
and the stars' gaze
to invent my future.

Today I will take the time to be happy
and will leave my footprints and my presence
in the hearts of others.

Today, I invite you to begin a new season
where we can dream
that everything we undertake is possible,
and we fulfill it with joy and dignity.

# -2-
# C>E: Results vs. Reasons
# Which side of the equation are you on?

Let's talk about cause and effect.

Are you interested in results, or the reasons you don't have the results you want?

Many motivators talk about empowerment, and sometimes we don't know what it is that they're actually talking about, or how we can actually get it. I mean, you might read several books or hear many speakers promoting this buzzword. When you're done reading or listening, you might expect to really comprehend what empowerment is, but you're left with gaping holes in your understanding. You may be pumped up, but confused about where you're really going or how to get there.

By the end of this chapter, you will know what empowerment is, and how to get it!

**Take Control of Your Bottom Line**
What is empowerment? Empowerment is taking the results over the reasons **every time**. Example: A diehard Falcons fan, season ticket holder, (me) goes to a game with her family. Before we entered the game, we decided that our goal or result was to have fun. It

was our individual responsibility. Whether the Falcons won or not could not impact our fun. We get in the game and watch the Falcons lose 45-17. This could have been devastating!

Regardless, we still enjoyed the tailgating, the company, the time with family and friends, and the fabulous food. What was the result? We empowered ourselves to be happy no matter what. We stayed on the cause side of the equation. I won't say we weren't disappointed, but we didn't allow something outside of us to effect our bottom line.

## C>E = Empowerment
Be honest with yourself...are you about results or are you about reasons?

Over the last week, how many instances did you offer reasons for not completing a task? When you offered these reasons (or some people might call them excuses), did that change the outcome of the situation?

*Excuses... excuses are the tools of incompetence which build monuments of nothing.*

If you have heard this, you are probably aware of the impact of your excuses. Let's bottom-line it...excuses amount to nothing. You either did it, or you didn't. Let's take this a step further and examine how the equation C>E can be used to empower and consequently change your life. That's right – change your life!

Cause and effect (C and E) puts **you** in the driver's seat. It allows you to take control and to be responsible for your actions. You will no longer have an external locus of control; instead, you will have an internal compass. This internal compass ultimately empowers you.

## Conscious Recording

When things happen (and they will happen), how you decide to view the situation has a direct impact on how the situation is recorded in your memory. Each person receives about 2 million bytes of information per second (bps). Of that 2 million bps, we can only pay attention to 134 bps. So if you really think about it, more information is being presented than we can really process. When you decide consciously what information you pay attention to, and how you allow that information to impact you, you allow yourself to be on the cause side of the equation.

## Choose Peace

For example, imagine yourself getting onto the highway. For many of us this event happens often. As soon as you make the turn to get on the highway, you notice there is heavy traffic. At that moment, you make a choice. The choice at that moment is to be upset or to be at peace with the traffic. You can make the decision to be at peace by recognizing that there is a purpose, at that point, for where you are. Now, there are other choices you can make about the traffic as well. One choice is to become frustrated, and allow all of the reasons you need to be somewhere else begin to frustrate you. You can allow that time in the car to literally impact your whole day negatively. You can sit in the traffic, angry and bitter. You can think of all the reasons this has happened. You'll get to work and be upset, and you in turn will affect the first person you come in contact with. Your energy, in turn, effects their day. This trickles throughout the day until the end of the day when you're right back in traffic.

I'm sure you're asking, "How I can be on the cause side with an event I did not cause?" It's your belief about the event that changes the event itself. Your belief can reframe the event in a more empowering light. If we took this same scenario and approached it from the cause side of the event, once you got onto the highway and you saw the traffic, you would have immediately taken a deep breath and began to determine how you could make the best out of the situation. For example, you could be overjoyed that you now have time to listen to powerful motivational speakers on audio!

I know, believe me, I know that this is different thinking from what you're used to. It will take an open mind for this to work. Here's the question for you. Are you getting the results that you want? I ask you, what side of the equation are you on? I can tell you if change your thinking, you will change your world.

**Choices and Being "On Cause"**
Every second of the day, you make a choice. You can choose to be happy, or you can choose to be sad, angry, frustrated, or upset. What choice are you making?

I hear from my clients "Dr. Cherry, you're always happy." They say "I can't be that way because I'm manic depressive, I'm bi polar, I'm gay, I've been raped, etc." My response to them is "every second – every second, I make the choice, and you can too. Can't you?" People like to believe that others (particularly people in my field) wake up in the morning and always have good days. Let me be the first to tell you (if you haven't heard this before), that is absolutely not true. I wake up in the morning and **create** a good day. I wake up in the morning and choose to be on the cause side of the equation. At any point, if I find myself coming up with reasons (my heart's been broken, I don't have enough this or that), then I force myself back to the results. I force myself back to the cause side.

There's nothing magical about the cause side of the equation. What is magical about this type of empowerment is you can do it. And you will, won't you?

# Results vs. Reasons

Either you have results or you have reasons. Be honest which do you have? Do you have the results you want or do you have lots of reasons for not having them?

**C>E Quiz**
If you are late for any event what explanation would you use?

1)    Traffic or another excuse
2)    Apologize and take responsibility

If someone promised to provide you with information and they didn't would you find the information yourself or blame the other person for your lack of success?

1)    Blame the other person
2)    Get it done

If you were cut off in traffic would you get over it in a few minutes or a few hours?

1)    Few minutes
2)    Few hours

Do you find your self waiting on others before you can achieve results?

1)    Yes
2)    No

Do you blame others for your mood?

1)    Do you say things like "she made me mad"; "he made me angry"
2)    Do you take responsibility for your mood

Do you find yourself being the victim often?
1)      Things always happen to me
2)      I am never a victim


If you answered selected number one to one or more of these you do use excuses and consequently you might not be getting the results you desire. Remember, you either have results or reasons. They do not take reasons at the bank, do they? You really must have results to be successful. And you do want success, don't you?

**List the excuses you made today**

_____
_____
_____
_____
_____


**List the results you received today**

_____
_____
_____
_____
_____
_____
_____
_____
_____

C>E:  Results vs. Reasons

# What Choices Do You Make?
Author Unknown

Michael is the kind of guy you love to hate.

He is always in a good mood and always has something positive to say.

When someone would ask him how he was doing, would reply, "If I were any better, I would be twins!"

He was a natural motivator.

If an employee was having a bad day, Michael was there telling the employee how to look on the positive side of the situation.

Seeing this style really made me curious, so one day I went up to Michael and asked him, "I don't get it! You can't be a positive person all of the time. How do you do it?" Michael replied, "Each morning I wake up and say to myself, you have two choices today.  You can choose to be in a good mood or ... you can choose to be in a bad mood.  I choose to be in a good mood.  Each time something bad happens, I can choose to be a victim or...I can choose to learn from it. I choose to learn from it.

Every time someone comes to me complaining, I can choose to accept their complaining or... I can point out the positive side of life. I can choose the positive side of life. "

"Yeah, right, it's not that easy," I protested.

"Yes, it is," Michael said. "Life is all about choices. When you cut away all the junk, every situation is a choice. You choose how you react to situations. You choose how people affect your mood. You choose to be in a good mood or bad mood. The bottom line: It's your choice how you live your life."

I reflected on what Michael said. Soon thereafter, I left the Tower Industry to start my own business. We lost touch, but I often thought about him when I made a choice about life instead of reacting to it.

Several years later, I heard that Michael was involved in a serious accident, falling some 60 feet from a communications tower. After 18 hours of surgery and weeks of
intensive care, Michael was released from the hospital with rods placed in his back. I saw Michael about six months after the accident. When I asked him how he was, he
replied. "If I were any better, I'd be twins. Wanna see my scars?" I declined to see his wounds, but I did ask him what had gone through his mind as the accident took place.

"The first thing that went through my mind was the well-being of my soon to be born daughter," Michael replied. "Then, as I lay on the ground, I remembered that I had two choices: I could choose to live or... I could choose to die. I chose to live."

"Weren't you scared? Did you lose consciousness?" I asked.

Michael continued, "...the paramedics were great. They kept telling me I was going to be fine. But when they wheeled me into the ER and I saw the expressions on the faces of the doctors and nurses, I got really scared. In their eyes, I read "he's a dead man. I knew I needed to take action."

"What did you do?" I asked.

"Well, there was a big burly nurse shouting questions at me," said Michael. "She asked if I was allergic to anything.

"Yes, I replied." The doctors and nurses stopped working as they waited for my reply. I took a deep breath and yelled, "Gravity."

Over their laughter, I told them, "I am choosing to live. Operate on me as if I am alive, not dead."

Michael lived, thanks to the skill of his doctors, but also because of his amazing attitude. I learned from him that every day we have the choice to live fully.

Attitude, after all, is everything.

Therefore do not worry about tomorrow, for tomorrow will worry about itself. Each day has enough trouble of its own. After all today is the tomorrow you worried about yesterday.

# The Power of Positive Thinking

One day my nephew came to a leadership development retreat with me. He was extremely excited because for the first time, he was able to see the type of work that I do. He was able to see people actually inspired to make a change in their lives. After the seminar, we decided to go for a bite to eat. While we were eating, he steered the conversation to what I did this summer. I told him about the experience of breaking a board with my bare hands. He looked at me incredulously and said, "Auntie, *you* broke a board?" And I assured him I did. Later, when he went to my office, he actually saw the (2 ply) wooden board laying in two pieces on my shelf. He was in shock that his aunt, with no martial arts training, could break a board with her hands. He pressed me "How did you do that?" I replied, "Beege, do you remember telling me that you knew everything? And that everything was inside your head? I told you you were correct. Well when you really think about it, I didn't break the board with my hands, I broke the board with my mind."

## Breaking the Barriers and Breaking the Board

I remember it like it was yesterday. I was in a room at an NLP seminar with 60 other people. The noise permeated the room – I mean it was *everywhere.* There was music, people cheering, applause. It was pretty much a party. Amidst the cheers and chants, brave souls in the group were stepping up to the wooden boards and breaking them one by one. Cheers and applause greeted each success.  As I watched them, I suddenly had the feeling that said it was my turn.  I took my board and went to the center of the room. I put it on the stand and got ready to break it. The noise seemed to crescendo.  I got into position and attempted to break the board. Boom. The board didn't break! But I felt as though my hand did.

I stepped back for a moment and went inside of myself. I connected with my source and all of the noise in the room disappeared. I got back into position and I closed my eyes. I summoned the strength in me, and the energy of the universe to break that board.  When I opened my eyes, the board was broken.

At that moment, I knew there were absolutely no obstacles I could not conquer using my inner strength, energy from God, and love from the universe.  You might ask, what would be the difference between the first time and the second time?  I'm going to tell you – the difference was the power in my mind. You see, the first time, I was focused externally on all the things going on around me.  To be honest, I was even focused on "what if the board didn't break."  I was listening to the chaos and all the confusion and self-doubt, and I allowed all of that to clutter my mind.  Once I removed all of the clutter and channeled the energy positively, the board broke.

The experience reminds me of *Flow: The Psychology of Optimal Experience* by Mihaly Csikszentmihalyi. When you are in the zone, when you're connected to your source, you can break a board, you can move the chair, you can accomplish whatever you desire. When you're disconnected, you can't break the board, move the chair, or accomplish anything of serious value. There are a couple of lessons from this. The first is learn how to focus on what it is you actually want – not on what you don't want.

**Learn to Focus Positively**
Many of us go through our days spending hours at a time contemplating things that will never happen. We actually focus on negative things – negative consequences. If many of us had the opportunity to write a what-if book for ourselves, we might have several chapters. In other words, we block ourselves with "what if this" or "what if that" instead of focusing on what we really want. What is it that you really want to manifest? In order for it to manifest you have to truly believe it is possible. So to do this, you must create your own belief system.

There are many simple statements out there you may have heard like "birds of a feather flock together," "opposites attract," "money is the root of all evil," or "nice guys finish last." You accept these with ease, whether or not you should. What you have to do is create a belief for your life that "anything is possible." I didn't say, "Anything is possible, but what if (you fill in the blank) happens." I said anything is possible. Period. Instead of using the famous word "but," you really should say, "Anything is possible *and* here's what I'll do." You have to focus on what you want. Clearly. Focusing on what you want, you have to use language that is going to empower you.

Like my nephew believes, we have all the resources we need to be successful inside of us. Excellent! We are perfect. We might not be flawless, and that's okay. The language that we use has to support our having empowering thoughts. A common phrase illustrates this point. Many people say, "I am sorry." Anything that follows "I am" should be powerful, wonderful, abundant, and magnificent. Certainly, you can apologize, but "I am" should always be followed by positive words. This is using language to support our empowerment.

When you're thinking about positive things, the day actually is more positive. If right now, you were to think about a person you didn't particularly like, and in the next instant, think of someone you did like, the positive energy that comes from thinking of the latter person would much more empowering. Focusing on the one you dislike brings in negative energy, which can send you on a downward spiral. Which one do you prefer?

**Choosing to Change Your Mind**
One thing that we must realize is that you have to **do** something. You have to take the step. You have to create the belief system to support positive thinking. Positive thinking doesn't just happen – you have to *make* it happen. If you find yourself thinking negatively, **you** have to change your mind. And guess who has the power to change your mind? If I asked you, right now, to close your eyes and relax the muscles around your eyes, whose responsibility is it for you to

close your eyes? That's right, definitely *your* responsibility. It is also your responsibility to create the system that will allow you to think positively. If you are not happy, change your mind and change your focus. One thing you can do to help change your mind is to physically look up. Research shows that looking up will actually change your perspective. Another thing you can do easily is vary your language. One of my mentors, Dr. Norman Vincent Peale, says that merely mentioning words like tranquility, prosperity, and abundance throughout the day changes your outlook.

Many people think the grass is greener on the other side. The truth in the matter is, if you water and tend to your own grass, it will be just as green (if not greener). Sometimes watering your grass comes in the form of gratitude or positive thoughts. Every 60 seconds, you have the opportunity to choose. You choose to be happy, don't you? If you're not choosing it, whose responsibility is it?

The Power of Positive Thinking

**What is symbolic of your "board" in the story (for example: weight, relationship, money)?**

_____

_____

_____

_____

_____

_____

_____

_____

**What barriers are stopping you from breaking your board?**

_____

_____

_____

_____

_____

_____

_____

**How will you approach your board differently?**

_____

_____

_____

_____

_____

_____

# The Power of Positive Thinking

*The Final Analysis by Mother Teresa*

People are often unreasonable, illogical, and self-centered;

**...Forgive them anyway!**

If you are kind, people may accuse you of selfish, ulterior motives;

**...Be kind anyway!**

If you are successful, you will win some false friends and some true enemies;

**...Succeed anyway!**

If you are honest and frank, people may cheat you;

**...Be honest and frank anyway!**

What you spend years building, someone could destroy overnight;

**...Build anyway!**

If you find serenity and happiness, they may be jealous;

**...Be happy anyway!**

The good you do today, people will often forget tomorrow;

**...Do good anyway!**

Give the world the best you have, and it may never be enough;

**...Give the world the best you've got anyway!**

You see, in the final analysis, it is between you and God;

**...It was never between you and them anyway.**

# -4-
# Obstacles

If at first you don't succeed, try, try again. How many times have you heard this simple statement? How many times have you actually repeated this statement to someone else? Now let's really get down to it... how many times have you applied it to your life?

I think one of the most valuable lessons that an individual can learn comes from a toddler. If you have the opportunity to watch a toddler fall when no one else seems to be watching, you will be amazed how quickly he or she will get back up. There was a popular song featuring the lyrics, "We fall down, but we get up." This song is important for dealing with obstacles because you will fall down, but you will get up, won't you?

**Signs of Success**
Many people use obstacles as excuses to stop striving for what they want. In reality, the obstacle is confirmation that you are doing what it is you're supposed to be doing. You see the obstacle is there to test you – not to stop you. It is up to you to create ways to maneuver around the obstacle. Right now, if you wanted to get from your front door to the kitchen and a chair was blocking you, would you just turn around and walk away, or would you move the chair?

In life, things happen exactly like that. You may be

attempting to get from point A to point Z, and the number three appears and you stop. In your mind, the number three doesn't fit with the alphabet, so you convince yourself that this is a sign that you're doing something incorrectly. This could not be further from the truth. The only sign in that scenario is that you didn't want to do it anyway. You conveniently created an excuse as to why God or the universe doesn't want you to complete the task. The truth is, God and the universe are infinitely abundant. What God and the universe would like for you to do is to look inside yourself, get the resources they have provided, and move the chair (or the number three). Essentially, you need to move out of your own way. Please don't let God be the excuse.

## Facing Fear with Faith

In the book *A Course in Miracles*, the scribe, Helen Schucman, lets us know that fear is not of God. Using God to justify your fear or your inadequacy is not acceptable. You see God gave man (woman) a mind. With that mind, infinite resources are available. I don't know about your God, but my God isn't sitting up there creating blocks for me. My God is constantly opening doors. Determination and persistence are the things that move obstacles. Your faith is what causes obstacles to disappear. If an obstacle isn't moving, it's really because you don't have the faith to move it. You are allowing fear to block you from prosperity, abundance, and your magnificence.

## Move That Chair!

Let's examine this for a moment. What is the last thing

you really wanted and didn't get? Think about it and write it down. Ask yourself why you gave up. What prevented you from moving forward? Now as you think about it, what other alternatives were available to you? If we were to go back to the chair example, perhaps I could have stood on the chair, climbed over the chair, moved the chair to the side, carried the chair away – several solutions were possible. If I turn away, my solution was to give up and say, "It wasn't for me." I am requesting that you **move** the chairs in your life.

The obstacles are going to keep coming. The obstacles are actually confirmation that you are on the correct path. Think about it – when you turn away from the chair, you don't gain the knowledge of learning to move the chair. What you actually gain is a medal in fear and insecurity. Congratulations. Each time you face an obstacle, you learn about your character. You learn and understand your strength, and you step out on your faith. Get what it is you really want! In order to achieve it, you absolutely must believe it. Making excuses for why you can't get it clearly shows that you don't believe it's possible. Faith is the substance of things hoped for...the evidence of things unseen. When you have faith, when you believe in yourself, you can do anything.

**Lessons from Obstacles**
There is a lesson to learn from every obstacle. When you don't complete the task, the obstacle appears somewhere else in another form. You see in life, we have tests. You will keep taking the test until you pass it. Not meeting the obstacle head on is only buying you

time until you meet it again. What will you do the next time? Take a few moments and think about an obstacle. If you were to be confronted with it today, how would you handle it, now?

There's an old proverb that says in order to make an omelet, you have to break an egg. In order to move forward, you're going to have to move the chair. The bottom line is there are things in life that you were created to do. The first time you took a step, it might have been a little wobbly and you might have even fallen. But the next time you took a step, it was more solid. Eventually you took more steps, and then you were actually walking. After walking you were running. You see, you grew stronger and you grow stronger with obstacles as well.

You have to believe that you have the strength necessary to successfully overcome the obstacles. If you don't believe it, the obstacle will appear to get bigger and more impossible to overcome. Actually, it might even start to laugh at you. Obstacles are bullies. You give them power by choosing to be afraid and choosing to do nothing. If you were to get in the face of the obstacle and challenge it, you would realize that the obstacle really doesn't even exist. It would just take off running.

If you don't believe me, why don't you just try it? Walk up to your obstacle and tell it there is only one power in the universe and that power is love. Tell it you believe in your ability to achieve your goal. You see that's really what it's about...it's about your ability to achieve your goal in spite of. A wise person once said "the things that don't kill you make you stronger." The confidence and power that comes from moving each chair builds character and deepens your faith. All of this ensures you will be successful in challenging your next obstacle.

So, take the step.

## Don't Just Stand There...

You might be saying to yourself it's not the perfect time. As you continue to look ahead and you see that the chairs in your life aren't parting like the Red Sea, realize you will never learn how to part the Red Sea until you successfully deal with the little obstacles first. There is no such thing as a perfect time other than right now.

## Knocking Out the "No"

You probably watched the movie *Rocky* (one of the several), but did you know that it took Sylvester Stallone over seven years before he could get his screenplay in the hands of a director? Even after the director and producer had it, they told Stallone that he would never be successful in the movie, and the only way they were going to make the film was if Robert Redford played the role. Now you might see that as an obstacle. By his own account, Stallone was broke. He was offered $100,000 for *Rocky* if he agreed not to star in the movie. Stallone said no thank you and he continued on his path until he found a company that would support his vision. The story today is history – it's rare for you to see anyone from the 80s generation that has not at least heard of *Rocky,* and the series has made millions.

## Don't Blame God, Thank God
Now what if Rocky walked away saying, "God said it wasn't meant to be." You see my view on God is that God gives you faith. You have the opportunity today to have everything in this world because you are a child of God. My God is not in the business of stopping you from moving forward. Be honest. You know and I know that God has the power to make all things possible, so you need another excuse for not moving the chair. Don't blame God, because God is the fundamental reason why you can. The only reason it's not for you today is because you don't want it today. If you wanted it, you would make it happen. You would create a way for it to happen.

When you take the first step, God will take the next. In 1997, I had a life-changing experience. My grandmother was faced with what many of us would call an obstacle. She was in the hospital and I went to visit her. When I arrived, my grandmother was in an enormous amount of pain. However, I couldn't tell that from her. As I walked toward her, she put on a smile that I can still see to this day. After she smiled at me, she turned away and made a face. I could tell she was really hurting. What my grandmother said during this time are words I'll never forget. From all of this pain my grandmother said "Thank you God." I was in shock. This is bigger than a chair, this is major, and she said "Thank you God." She said to God "I have been your faithful servant. and I am now ready to come home." She had faith beyond any type of faith that I even knew existed. To be on your deathbed, in pain, to be able to smile and still have faith... I knew then – these things we call obstacles aren't really obstacles at all. Faith makes the obstacle disappear. My grandmother believed it, and she modeled this behavior. She could have very easily blamed God or other people, but she said, "Thank you God." She asked God, and she believed that God would help her remove the obstacle, and He did.

**Ask and Receive**
Obstacles, or so-called obstacles come in different forms. Sometimes they are in the form of voices. The owner of the Kentucky Fried Chicken franchises heard "no" over 1,200 times before he was able to get one person to agree to just listen to him. When I wanted to start my own business, voices kept blocking my way. "Are you sure you can do that with the economy this way?" "Don't you have a great job with benefits?" Voices like that are definitely obstacles. Needless to say, I moved those obstacles and started my own business. One week in particular, after I stopped procrastinating, I exposed a rainbow of good fortune.


When you start your own business, you are everyone from the janitor to the CEO. There was a conference I wanted to attend in Philadelphia. The CEO (me) knew the money wasn't there. Wanting to go to a conference without the funds can be an obstacle. I decided to challenge the obstacle, and I sent the message to the universe that I was serious about this challenge. Right after I sent the message, one of my prospective clients called me and asked if I wanted to represent his company at the conference.

I attended that conference in Philly and that wasn't my only victory. When I arrived in Philly, I took the subway. As I was exiting, an elderly lady caught my eye. As she walked, I noticed we were headed in the same direction. I slowed down to be in sync with her. We took the elevator together, and once we made it to the main level, she asked me if I wanted to share a cab with her. Now people who have fear in them may have been afraid. Because fear is not of God in my model of the world, I shared the cab with her. In this cab ride, this lady began to tell me that all of my dreams were going to come true...that I would be successful in my business. As I sat there in complete shock, we arrived to my hotel and I began to pull my money out for the cab. She said to me, with a smile, "Your money is no good here. I have this."

I'm not sure how well I explained to you that I *didn't* have the funds to go to the conference, but what I had was the faith and the belief that I *would* go – no matter what. I won't tell you everything that happened to me on that trip, but I will tell you this – I left Atlanta with $70 and I came home with $70. People were constantly placed in my path to help me to achieve the goal.

You see I took the step – I moved the chair. I had the faith and I believed. By stepping out on that faith I was able to increase my faith and grow stronger. I could have just as easily procrastinated and sat at home complaining and saying "it's just not my time." Had I done that, I wouldn't have gotten the lesson nor would I have the story to give you today. Take the step...move the chair. This is what God wants you to do. And you can do that, can't you?

**What is the last thing you really wanted and did not get?**

_____

_____

_____

_____

_____

_____

_____

**What lesson did you learn from not getting it?**

_____

_____

_____

_____

_____

_____

**How will you get something you really want in the future?**

_____

_____

_____

_____

_____

_____

Obstacles
# "God Said No"

I asked God to take away my habit.
**God said, No.**
It is not for me to take away, but for you to give it up.

I asked God to make my handicapped child whole.
**God said, No.**
His spirit is whole, his body is only temporary

I asked God to grant me patience.
**God said, No.**
Patience is a byproduct of tribulations;
it isn't granted, it is learned.

I asked God to give me happiness.
**God said, No.**
I give you blessings; Happiness is up to you.

I asked God to spare me pain.
**God said, No.**
Suffering draws you apart from worldly cares
and brings you closer to me.

I asked God to make my spirit grow.
**God said, No.**
You must grow on your own,
but I will prune you to make you fruitful.

I asked God for all things that I might enjoy life.
**God said, No.**
I will give you life, so that you may enjoy all things.

I asked God to help me LOVE others, as much as He loves me. God said...Ahhhh, finally you have the idea.

# -5-
# There Is No Failure, Only Feedback

There really is no failure...there is only feedback. Many of us, including me (and probably only me ☺), use excuses and fear as blockers. I can readily tell you 10 reasons why this book isn't done yet. Instead of me thinking negatively, I except the results and realize I am where I am. I pay attention to the message or the sign – the feedback.

**You Do Better When You Know Better**
Many times we'll have a great idea and not know exactly what to do. Because things didn't turn out exactly the way we wanted them to, we view the situation and/or ourselves as a failure. I am here to tell you that you didn't fail. You did then what you knew how to do. When you knew better, you did better. Look at each situation in your life as an experience and an opportunity. If it didn't go exactly the way you wanted it to go, that is not failure. That is an opportunity. Along with that opportunity, we get feedback. The feedback allows us to take the scenario and improve it. How wonderful!

What I want you to do is to create a belief that enables you to be gentle with yourself. I would like you, today, to accept your current situation and embrace it. Instead of making those 10 excuses that I really could make about the book, I realize that it wasn't time for the book to come out. We have to learn that everything on this earth is exactly as it should be. If you didn't get that promotion that you wanted, don't think of it as a failure. Think of it as an opportunity. Think of it as feedback. If you didn't get the husband, wife, boyfriend, car, shoes that you wanted, don't look at it as failure. Look at it as feedback. Excellent! Get the lesson and move forward!

## Make the Grade

Life is really about the lesson. It's about the individual experiences. Each experience (or test as I like to call them) gives us information (feedback) for the next test. Right now, as you're reading this book, you're being prepared for your next test. This morning as you drove to school or work, you were being prepared for your next test. Everything that happens truly happens for a reason. Your goal should be to get the feedback from the situation and incorporate that feedback into your future actions.

Example: Imagine you were in school and you turned in a paper. The paper was returned to you with an "F," and with the "F" you also received constructive feedback. You can more than likely take that feedback and turn that "F" into a "C," a "B," or an "A" paper. Essentially that's what we do in life. Each obstacle, each challenge we face is like that paper. The responses that we get from the people we come in contact with are the remarks from the paper. You have the opportunity to take the feedback, incorporate it, and literally change your behavior everyday.

**Get the Lesson**
There is no failure, only feedback. It is inevitable that we focus on the wholeness that exists within us. It is imperative that we recognize that just because things don't go exactly as we wanted them to go at that time, doesn't mean that we failed. What it means is that you have (learned) a valuable lesson. *Get the lesson.* Sometimes we are so focused on the fact that we didn't reach our goals, we fail to get the lesson. Right now, I would like for you to think back to a time you thought you failed. What I would like for you to do is ask yourself what were the valuable lessons that you learned? What was it that you now know today, that you would not have learned had it not been for that experience? See the truth is, *there is no failure, there is only feedback.* There is only an opportunity for you to get back on the horse. There is only the opportunity for you to gain the information you need to continue traveling down the correct path.

**Failure=Victory**
As you look back on your greatest challenges and what you might have considered to be a failure, you will see the greatest victories of your life. The beautiful thing about recognizing the feedback is that it helps you to move beyond the fear. Remember that fear is not of God. As you move toward what it is you truly want, you can't fail because there *is no failure.* You can move easily and effortlessly toward that goal. What you will realize is that by moving toward that goal, you will get

the feedback that will help you reach your goal successfully. No matter how hard you try, you can't fail. When things don't go as you planned or hoped, there is feedback and a lesson for you to learn. As you think about those so-called failures, ensure that your lessons you get are about *you*. Have the lesson be positive, future-based, and about yourself. Get the lesson and let go of the concept of "I failed."

The most successful people in the world will tell you that right before their greatest success came their greatest defeat. Just because things are not going your way today doesn't mean you are failing. What it might mean is that you're not listening to the feedback. We get feedback all the time. It is up to us to pay attention and incorporate it, so we can move out of our own way and be even more successful. Can you imagine how empowering it would be for you, if today, right now, you decided you *couldn't* fail? One of the questions I ask my coaching clients, and I'm asking you today, what would you do if you knew you couldn't fail? Many of us are so afraid of failure that we fail to do anything. We sit back and watch time dwindle while someone else is out there learning lessons and succeeding.

**Find the "Right" in the Middle of "Wrong"**
John Maxwell has a book called *Failing Forward*. He believes in turning mistakes into stepping stones for success. One of the major things we have to do is separate ourselves from the event. You have to realize that you are not a failure. The situation turned out differently from your expectations. To be honest, the

situation turned out as it should have. When we are faced with obstacles, it is up to us to change our mind on how we view them. Think about finding what is right in *every* situation. What was right? As you look at what went right, you will change your opinion of the situation. There is no need, ever, to beat yourself up. You are doing the best you can with what you have. And guess what? If you are not doing your best, you will continue to get that feedback until you *are* doing your best. When you are in a situation, and it doesn't turn out the way you'd like, pause, take a deep breath, and say to yourself (out loud), "Excellent! Self, I did then what I knew how to do. Now that I know better, I'll do better." Pay close attention to the feedback. If you need to do something differently, be willing to do it.

It wasn't an accident that one of the top gospel songs in 2000 was also at the top of the pop charts. The song "We Fall Down, But We Get Up" has a theme we can all relate to. In life, you might fall down...it doesn't make you a failure. Take the feedback, learn the lesson, and get back up!

There Is No Failure, Only Feedback

**How specifically will you use this lesson on feedback?**

_____

_____

_____

_____

_____

**What are some great (positive) lessons that you have gained from unsuccessful experiences?**

_____

_____

_____

_____

_____

_____

_____

**What lessons have you learned for the future?**

_____

_____

_____

_____

_____

_____

_____

# What have you learned about your self as a result of these lessons?

_____

_____

_____

_____

_____

_____

_____

_____

## Teddy's Story
## Author Unknown

Jean stood in front of her fifth-grade class on the very first day of school in the fall and told the children a lie. Like most teachers, she looked at her pupils and said that she loved them all the same, that she would treat them all alike. And that was impossible because there in front of her, slumped in his seat on the third row, was a boy named Teddy Stoddard.

Mrs. Thompson had watched Teddy the year before and noticed he didn't play well with the other children, that his clothes were unkempt and that he constantly needed a bath. And Teddy was unpleasant. It got to the point during the first few months that she would actually take delight in marking his papers with a broad red pen, making bold X's and then marking the F at the top of the paper biggest of all. Because Teddy was a sullen little boy, no one else seemed to enjoy him, either. At the school where Mrs. Thompson taught, she was required to review each child's records and put Teddy's off until last. When she opened his file, she was in for a surprise.

His first-grade teacher wrote, "Teddy is a bright, inquisitive child with a ready laugh. He does his work neatly and has good manners...he is a joy to be around."

His second-grade teacher wrote, "Teddy is an excellent student, well-liked by his classmates, but he is troubled because his mother has a terminal illness and life at home must be a struggle."

His third-grade teacher wrote, "Teddy continues to work hard but his mother's death has been hard on him. He tries to do his best but his father doesn't show much interest and his home life will soon affect him if some steps aren't taken."

Teddy's fourth-grade teacher wrote, "Teddy is withdrawn and doesn't show much interest in school. He doesn't have many friends and sometimes sleeps in class. He is tardy and could become a problem."

By now Mrs. Thompson realized the problem but Christmas was coming fast. It was all she could do, with the school play and all, until the day before the holidays began and she was suddenly forced to focus on Teddy Stoddard. Her children brought her presents, all in gay ribbon and bright paper, except for Teddy's, which was clumsily wrapped in the heavy, brown paper of a scissored grocery bag.

Mrs. Thompson took pains to open it in the middle of the other presents. Some of the children started to laugh when she found a rhinestone bracelet with some of the stones missing, and a bottle that was one-quarter full of cologne. She stifled the children's laughter when she exclaimed how pretty the bracelet was, putting it on, and dabbing some of the perfume behind the other wrist.

Teddy Stoddard stayed behind just long enough to say, "Mrs. Thompson, today you smelled just like my mom used to." After the children left she cried for at least an hour. On that very day, she quit teaching reading, and writing, and speaking. Instead, she began to teach *children*. Jean Thompson paid particular attention to one they all called "Teddy".

As she worked with him, his mind seemed to come alive. The more she encouraged him, the faster he responded. On days there would be an important test, Mrs. Thompson would remember that cologne. By the end of the year he had become one of the smartest children in the class and...well, he had also become the "pet" of the teacher who had once vowed to love all of her children exactly the same.

A year later she found a note under her door, from Teddy, telling her that of all the teachers he'd had in elementary school, she was his favorite. Six years went by before she got another note from Teddy. He then wrote that he had finished high school, third in his class, and she was still his favorite teacher of all time. Four years after that, she got another letter, saying that while things had been tough at times, he'd stayed in school, had stuck with it, and would graduate from college with the highest of honors.

He assured Mrs. Thompson she was still his favorite teacher.

Then four more years passed and yet another letter came. This time he explained that after he got his bachelor's degree, he decided to go a little further. The letter explained that she was still his favorite teacher but that now his name was a little longer. The letter was signed, Theodore F. Stoddard, M.D.

The story doesn't end there.

You see, there was yet another letter that Spring. Teddy said he'd met this girl and was to be married. He explained that his father had died a couple of years ago and he was wondering...well, if Mrs. Thompson might agree to sit in the pew usually reserved for the mother of the groom.

You'll have to decide yourself whether or not she wore that bracelet, the one with several rhinestones missing.

But, I bet on that special day, Jean Thompson smelled just like...well, just like she smelled many years before, on that last day of school, before the Christmas Holiday began.

You never can tell what type of impact you may make on another's life by your actions or lack of action. Sometimes just a smile on the street to a passing stranger can make a difference we could never imagine.

Wouldn't it be nice if we all could have this impact on people?

We do.

-6-
# Respect Everybody's Model of the World

"If I do not want what you want, please try not to tell me that my want is wrong. Or if I believe other than you, at least pause before you correct my view. Or if my emotion is less than yours, or more, given the same circumstances, try not to ask me to feel more strongly or weakly. Or yet if I act, or fail to act, in the manner of your design for action, let me be. I do not, for the moment at least, ask you to understand me. That will come only when you are willing to give up changing me into a copy of you.

I may be your spouse, your parent, your offspring, your friend, your professor, your relative or your colleague. If you will allow me any of my own wants, or emotions, or beliefs, or actions, then you open yourself, so that some day these ways of mine might not seem so wrong, and might finally appear to you as right – for me. To put up with me is the first step of understanding me. Not that you embrace my ways as right for you, but you are no longer irritated or disappointed with me for my waywardness. And in understanding me you might come to prize my differences from you, and far from seeking to change me, preserve and even nurture those differences."

This powerful excerpt is from *Please Understand Me* by Kiersey and Bates, and it's the perfect introduction to this lesson. One of the easiest ways for you to move out of your own way is to realize that everyone doesn't think like you. Zig Ziglar says, "People don't care how much you know, until they know how much you care about them." Each person is unique. As the real life Rain Man, Kim Peek says, "people are different." When you come in contact with someone whose belief is different from yours, realize that they actually have a right to feel or think that way. It is a beautiful experience to understand that peace is much more important than being right. In *A Course in Miracles*, we find the concept "I can choose peace over this." The magnificent learning from this is that you have the opportunity to choose. Once you develop value and respect for the other person's model of the world, you will be able recognize your ego (the part that separates you from the universe) always wants to be right. Instead of allowing your ego to control you, you will come to respect, even if not agree with, models that frame the world differently.

**Ego vs. Peace**
An amazing thing happened to me in the middle of a debate. During the debate I remembered to have respect for the other person's model of the world, and I chose peace. Imagine this – we are in the middle of an actual debate. My opponent had just finished speaking and it

was my turn to rebut. I was all set to attack and reiterate my point, but I felt I needed to try something different. In that moment, I looked the individual in the eye and I said, "You are correct." The neurological messages on my opponent's face were remarkable. He appeared shocked and perplexed and then continued to argue his point. I learned the lesson at that moment. The lesson for me was that person had a right to believe whatever he wanted to believe. Forcing my view didn't show respect for his model of the world. I didn't allow my ego to control me. This is true most of the time. I'm not perfect... I, too, trip up and fall down. When I do fall down, it's typically because my ego is interested in being right and not in searching for peace.

Hear me out. There are situations in life when you are driving with green lights ahead. As you cruise, you notice the person with the red light is still coming toward you. In that moment, I ask you, is it important to be dead right? Always remember, you can choose peace. You don't have to prove yourself to anybody. I can't tell you how many years it took for me to understand that lesson.

**Who's the Boss?**
One of my students challenged me in class an entire semester. No matter what I said, she disagreed. Had that happened early in my teaching career, I might have gone toe to toe. I might have done everything in my power to show her who's the boss and how much information I had. Because I had learned to respect her model of the world and to choose peace, every time she challenged me, I looked at her and told her she was

correct. The truth is, your perception is your reality. What you think is true, is actually true…for you. It would be pretty difficult for me to tell you that you don't have a headache if you did. You would probably say, "How do you know what I have?" The truth of the matter is I don't know.

**A Mile in My Shoes**
As we look at life, we view it through our very own lenses. It's pretty impossible for you, if you're a man reading this book in the United States, to have the same experience as say, a woman who may be reading the book in Japan. People see things differently. We see life based on our experiences. You woke up this morning in your body. In that same body today, you have spent every minute of the day. Nobody else out there knows what you went through today. Nobody else understands exactly how you came to frame your model of the world. I can only accept your model.

The same student asked me once, "Don't you get frustrated when you're not right?" I told her that being right doesn't help anyone. What helps a person is understanding him or her. The whole point of this section is learning to understand that other people might not think exactly like you and that is perfectly okay. One of the best tools used to divide people is actually religion. We suppose if someone doesn't think exactly like we do, his or her belief is wrong. What I think is his or her belief is simply different. It doesn't have to be wrong, and it doesn't have to be for you.

You see, it's not always about *us*. Sometimes, it's about us helping others. Sometimes we can best help others through compassion and understanding. You don't have to walk a mile in someone else's shoes, but it might not hurt. Respect everyone's model world.

**What do you see in the pictures?**

_____
_____
_____
_____
_____
_____
_____
_____

**Is it possible for others to see something different? Can you both be correct?**

_____

_____

_____

_____

_____

_____

_____

**Can you tell me what the picture above is? Sure you can it is from my model of the world. Everybody knows what is in my head, right? When you know what it is email me. I would love to hear what you think it is.**

_____

_____

_____

_____

_____

_____

_____

**List things you can do to be sure to acknowledge the other persons model of the world.**

_____

_____

_____

_____

_____

_____

_____

_____

_____

_____

_____

_____

_____

_____

_____

_____

_____

_____

_____

_____

_____

_____

_____

_____

# The Cookie Thief
## by Valerie Cox

A woman was waiting at an airport one night,
With several long hours before her flight.
She hunted for a book in the airport shops.
Bought a bag of cookies and found a place to drop.

She was engrossed in her book but happened to see,
That the man sitting beside her, as bold as could be.
Grabbed a cookie or two from the bag in between,
Which she tried to ignore to avoid a scene.

So she munched the cookies and watched the clock,
As the gutsy cookie thief diminished her stock.
She was getting more irritated as the minutes ticked by,
Thinking, "If I wasn't so nice, I would blacken his eye."

With each cookie she took, he took one too,
When only one was left, she wondered what he would
do.
With a smile on his face, and a nervous laugh,
He took the last cookie and broke it in half.

He offered her half, as he ate the other,
She snatched it from him and thought... oooh, brother.
This guy has some nerve and he's also rude,
Why he didn't even show any gratitude!

She had never known when she had been so galled,
And sighed with relief when her flight was called.
She gathered her belongings and headed to the gate,
Refusing to look back at the thieving ingrate.

She boarded the plane, and sank in her seat,
Then she sought her book, which was almost complete.
As she reached in her baggage, she gasped with surprise,
There was her bag of cookies, in front of her eyes.

If mine are here, she moaned in despair,
The others were his, and he tried to share.
Too late to apologize, she realized with grief,
That she was the rude one, the ingrate, the thief.

How many times in our lives,
have we absolutely known
that something was a certain way,
only to discover later that
what we believed to be true ... was not?

# -7-
# The Man and the Saw

## Excuses, Stress, and Worry

One thing that has never worked for me is the whole concept of excuses. I've just never been very fond of excuses. And I believe that as you start to think about creating excuses, you'll start to realize that all you're doing is creating stress. Stress is definitely a blocker to success. My mentor, Tad James, says we spend most of our lives worrying about things that will never happen. I heard a speaker, Keith Harrell, recently say, "worry is a negative form of meditation." When people say *don't worry*, I know it's easier said than done, but worrying causes anxiety for something that might not ever happen.

I want to invite you to think about and realize that no matter what it is you want to do, you have the power to do it. You have all the resources inside of you to be successful. It doesn't matter who you are, doesn't matter where you are.

## Set Goals and Challenge Obstacles

My uncle recently went to my cousin's house, and he decided that he was going to cut down a tree. This was very important to him because the tree was dead and in a potentially dangerous place. All it would take is an ice storm to bring that tree crashing down with disastrous results. If you've ever cut down a tree, this might not seem like a big deal. But imagine cutting down a tree while having physical limitations. My uncle has prostate cancer. And to be honest my uncle really doesn't know that he has prostate cancer because he doesn't allow the cancer to rule him. If you were to call him right now he would say he was doing "fantastic" because mentally he is in control of his state of life. Now that's not to say that he isn't in pain, because I've had the opportunity to be in his presence before and I've seen him in pain. However, he wouldn't allow anything to block his ability and belief that he could overcome his pain.

## A Vision of Success

Well, my uncle had a vision that he was going to remove this tree no matter what. My cousin suggested hiring someone to remove the tree and he said no, I'm going to do it myself. So one Saturday he came to the house to tackle this tree. It was a serious tree, and with all of my health, and all of my might, and all of my strength, I would never, ever have considered cutting down this tree myself – especially with a manual saw. Yes, my uncle arrived prepared to conquer the tree with a manual saw. A manual saw.

## Mind Over Matter

He began the task of cutting down the tree. It took him some hours and some serious sweat, and he realized that the tree wasn't going down that day. Some branches did make it down though. My uncle was tired, in pain, and sweating profusely, however, he never once gave in to the belief that the tree wasn't going down eventually. I think the tree was probably pretty excited when it saw the manual saw thinking, hey, I get to stay around for a while. However, it didn't know what the power of determination, the power of the mind can actually accomplish.

So, a week passes and my uncle comes back. Again with the manual saw. It's round two for the tree. More sweat. More pain. More branches on the ground.

## Always Obstacles, Never Failure

The next week it was round three. He came with another tool this time. This time it was a chain saw. Even this was not without challenges. It was hard to start, then the engine flooded, I mean the obstacles were still there. Still, he kept to the task, and he was able to cut down more of the tree. Minutes later, the tree was completely down! However, this is still physical work, and he wasn't able to move all the branches of the tree exactly where he wanted for disposal.

So he came back yet another Saturday. And on the fourth Saturday, the tree was completely down, the branches were removed, and he had accomplished the task the way he envisioned it. Never, never did he imagine that because of the limitations other people projected onto him, that he was not going to be able to remove the tree. When you believe in yourself, no person living or unborn, has the ability to block that. If you believe that you can do something, it can be done.

## Life After Death

In 1991, my dad was actually diagnosed with a rare form of cancer. It was and is to this day one of the deadliest forms of cancer. Doctors gave him six months to live and they pretty much sent him home to die. They suggested he join a survivor group, made up of patients with this disease.

To date every person in that group died - except for one. That one person is my father. Now I have never had this conversation with my dad, but what I'll say is the reason my father is still living and will celebrate his 75th birthday very soon, (and this is 15 years post-prognosis), is because my father decided in his mind that he was going to live.

**Feeding the Body and the Soul**
My father and I have differing views on what is good to eat. My mother is arguably the best cook in the south (ok, in the world!) and she cooks traditional southern food. For as long as I can remember, my mother has always prepared a good, home-cooked meal for my father and me. When my father got the news of his cancer, he did not change his diet (as the doctors suggested). To be honest, at that time I couldn't see how continuing to eat chitterlings, collards, ox tails, etc. was going to keep him healthy. However, my dad decided that he was going to live! He was going to live and altering all of the things that had made him who he was wasn't something that he was willing to do. Occasionally he still even has his gin with lime juice. *He made a choice that he was going to live*, and that's really what cultivating your fruits is all about.

It's really about telling your mind, telling yourself, that you are going to live. Whatever it is that you are going through, you have the power inside, you have the resources available to you to be successful. All you need to do is move out of your own way.

If the only thing we have to fear is death, then we really don't have anything to fear. I will admit this concept is still hard for me to grasp, but I read a passage in the Bible that helped, Revelation 21:4, "He will wipe every tear from their eyes. There will be no more death or mourning or crying or pain, for the old order of things has passed away." As my Aunt Mattie says, death is one debt we will have to pay. As long as we are here, there is work to be done. One author says "the way you know your work isn't complete is because you are still alive."

**Live, Dream, and Succeed**
One day, you will pass on but until that day does come, live. Live your life. Stop worrying! Stop blocking your success with stress! Think about the man and the saw with advanced prostate cancer, still being able to envision a dream and to get it done. It doesn't matter what your dream is. It really doesn't. It just matters that you accomplish it. Martin Luther King, Jr. wasn't the only person who had a dream. You have a dream today as well, and every day that you succeed on a dream is a win. If your dream for today is to get up and wash your hair and you did it, congratulate yourself and I congratulate you too. You have succeeded today, and you will continue to succeed.

The Man and the Saw

## What trees will you cut down?

_____

_____

_____

_____

_____

_____

_____

_____

_____

_____

_____

_____

_____

_____

**Don't Quit**
**Author Unknown**

When things go wrong as they sometimes will;
When the road you're trudging seems all uphill;
When the funds are low, and the debts are high
And you want to smile, but have to sigh;
When care is pressing you down a bit-
rest if you must, but do not quit.

Success is failure turned inside out;
The silver tint of the clouds of doubt;
And you can never tell how close you are
It may be near when it seems so far;
So stick to the fight when you're hardest hit-
It's when things go wrong that you must not quit.

# High Maintenance vs. Knowing What You Want

In a scene from a famous movie, Sally was sitting in a restaurant with Harry ordering what she wanted – *exactly* what she wanted off the menu.

> "I'd like the chef's salad please, with the oil and vinegar on the side, and the apple pie a la mode."

The waitress confirms the order, to which Sally adds (in one breath):

> "But I'd like the pie heated, and I don't want the ice cream on top, I want it on the side, and I want strawberry if you have it, if not, then no ice cream, just whipped cream but only if it's real, if it's out of a can, then nothing."

The waitress, who appears to be in a state of shock asks, "Not even the pie?" To which Sally responds, "No, just the pie, but then not heated."

Many people view her actions as "high maintenance." I call that knowing what you want. Some people look at the menu and order what is there. Other people order what they want. The interesting thing is some people don't realize that just because it's not on the menu doesn't mean that they can't get it. You see many of us use the menu to limit our possibilities. We do this in life as well.

## Create Your Own Menu

A person creates a menu, and a person creates the menu based on what he or she thinks would be appealing. What you have to be prepared to do is *always* get what you want – no matter what (as long as it's good for you and not harmful to the universe). I remember growing up hearing statements like "nothing beats failure but a try," and this can be applied here. You don't know that you can do something until you ask. You don't know what's available to you until you try. It's really not about being high maintenance in a negative way. It's really about knowing what you want. If you know what you want, you should order exactly that. Here's the thing – you might not get it; however, you might. You never know until you try.

Look at life and think about the menu that is being presented to you now. Additionally, consider what you want that is not being presented. You actually have the opportunity to order what does not seem available. There is no law written that states you *have* to only order what's on the menu. Create your own! It really doesn't matter if you're ordering from McDonald's or the Cheesecake Factory…ask for what you want.

## Seek and Find

Life is really like a buffet (but keep it mind, it's still not limited to what's on the buffet). What I mean is, you really have the option to pick and choose what you want. Here's what separates the good from the great:

the great are resourceful. Once they have set their minds to it, they figure out a way to get it done. That's what I encourage you to do. I encourage you to constantly figure out ways to get things done. Let your mind continue to create new opportunities for you.

If you were listening to the traffic report and you heard there was an accident on the same path you were planning to take, you would consider an alternate route. That is an example of being resourceful. What you want to do is continue to find alternate routes. The title of the book is *Move Out of Your Own Way*. What you want to do is move over so you can be more successful. Continuously seek and find new paths and opportunities. You have to treat your life as though it were a computer. If you were to buy the top of the line computer today, six months later, that computer would no longer be the top model. When the computer was launched, the designers were already working on the next best thing. You need to work on the next best thing for you all the time.

**Cheese Please**
There's a great book called *Who Moved My Cheese?* by Spencer Johnson, M.D. At the end of the book, when you realize the cheese is always going to move, the question for you becomes: are you going to move with the cheese or not?

Some of us might think there's only one type of cheese. Those of us who are high maintenance will realize the cheese can be Swiss today, provolone tomorrow, and cheddar the next day. Every time we order it, we expect to have the cheese the way we want it. We create the resources to make that happen. That's what we all should do. You should always empower yourself to get what you want.

## Realize Your Resources

Zig Ziglar says you can get whatever you want if you help enough other people get what they want. I am by no means advocating that you get what you want at the expense of others. What I'm suggesting here is that you get what you want and you use and understand the resourceful mind, body, and spirit that you have available. Realize there are no limits to what you can do. Absolutely no limits. Whatever you believe, you can achieve. Someone else once said, whether you think you can or cannot, you are right. You see, half the battle is realizing that it's possible, and realizing that just because it hasn't been done or no one else is doing it, doesn't mean you cannot.

Can you imagine what people must have thought about the Wright Brothers? When they announced they planned to fly? I mean think about that. It was hard enough to think about driving, and now someone is saying they want to fly? The Wright Brothers didn't order what was already on the transportation menu; they ordered what they wanted. Think about the person who created TiVo. This person definitely looked beyond the menu. Any person who has been in contact with TiVo knows that television technology has been taken to the next level.

Hear me out. Ordering off the menu sometimes makes it more difficult. I remember being at a Steak 'n Shake recently and the sign there read "Special orders take time. Please allow time for your order to be prepared." When you order what's on the menu, it's easier for it to be prepared. When you order what you want, it may take a little bit longer, but the taste is so much sweeter. The reward is so much greater.

## The Motivation of No

Let me tell you a brief history of a Sony product. The product was actually created by an individual who was at home playing a video game with his daughter. As Ken Kutaragi played the game with his daughter, he was amazed at the lack of high quality graphics and sound effects in use, and he knew that the technology was available. He couldn't understand why such low quality was acceptable. Mr. Kutaragi went to the manufacturer of his daughter's unit, and said he had the capability to make their system one of the best ever. The company agreed to work with him. Right after he refined the technology and the unit, the company pulled out. He was left with lots of a hard work and a product that was clearly superior to any product on the market at that time.

He then turned to Sony. He looked at Sony's menu and realized that gaming was not present. He talked to just about every senior executive at Sony, and not one of them believed in his vision. As a matter of fact, they made comments like, "We do electronics, not games."

People started to ostracize him. There was one man in Sony, the leader at the time, who was willing to listen. He gave Mr. Kutaragi the smallest team, the smallest budget, and allowed him to work on the product. Mr. Kutaragi's team was ostracized, and they became the laughing stock of Sony. Mr. Kutaragi didn't stop because people laughed at him. He actually let "no" be his motivator.

When the product came on the market that we now know as the Sony PlayStation, Sony captured a huge market share. Now those same people who were sticking firmly to their menu actually owe this man a lot for increasing the value of their company. Does this make sense? This man did not let the menu limit him. He knew what he wanted and that's what he ordered. You can do this too, can't you? He was resourceful. He continued to move with the cheese. Now his daughter has a game she can play with the quality her father thought she deserved. High maintenance decisions pay off. Move out of your own way and get what it is you really want.

The next time you're out and you're looking at a menu, and you know you want something that isn't listed, ask for it anyway. Someone just might be able to create it for you. You'll never know if you don't ask.

## What would you like to order?

_____

_____

_____

_____

_____

_____

_____

## When will you place your order?

_____

_____

_____

_____

_____

_____

_____

## Persistence
### By: Calvin Coolidge

Nothing in the world can take the place of Persistence.

Talent will not; nothing is more common than unsuccessful men with talent.

Genius will not; unrewarded genius is almost a proverb.

Education will not; the world is full of educated failure.

Keep believing.

Keep trying.

Persistence and Determination alone are omnipotent.

# -9-
# Thinking Beyond the Box

We are only limited by our thoughts. One of the most difficult things for people to realize is that we are perfect. We might not be flawless, but we are perfect. The more we realize we are perfect, the more we are grounded in abundance instead of lack. Oftentimes we focus on our flaws and we let those flaws limit us. The most beautiful thing to realize is that you really are perfect. As you're reading this, some of you are questioning this. "I'm perfect?" Yes, you are. When my nephew was four years old, he told me he knew everything. I said, "Beege, you know everything?" He said, "Yes, it's all in my head." I thought about it and I looked at him, and I said, "You're 100% correct." He has all the resources to be successful inside of him, and we all do. It's amazing when a four year old realizes it.

There was a study done in a school system. In this study, a group of kindergarteners were asked if they thought they could sing. Over 95% of the kindergarteners thought they could. The same question was asked to seniors in high school. Less than 20% of them thought they could sing. The researchers went on to infer when we're young, we don't know what we don't know; we just believe we can. As we grow older, we hear people telling us what we can and cannot do.

We start to believe that something that is truly possible is now impossible.

## Be Visionary

We have the power to make things happen. Often, we are so blinded by what we think is *not* possible, we never see the possibilities. Helen Keller has two quotes that speak to this. The first one is: "A door never closes without a window being opened." We spend so much time looking at the closed door that we never see the window. The other quote was personal to her. Someone asked her what could be worse than being blind? She said having sight with no vision. That is a powerful statement. How many of us have sight, but no vision? We aren't sure what our next steps are, what we should be doing, or how to get to the next level. We think we're stuck without options.

Individuals are not the only ones guilty of this practice. Organizations fall into the same paradigm often. Because organizations are truly a collection of people, it is important for the people in the organization to think outside of the box to create new and exciting ways for change.

## A Lesson from the Postal Service

A few examples in history stand out in my mind where organizations were limited by lack of vision. The first example is the United States Postal Service. The Postal Service was guilty of what Janis calls "groupthink." We might call it institutional thinking. What do you think happened to the Postal Service in the last ten years? Why do you think they haven't been as profitable as in times past? The Postal Service believed it was the only outlet for mail delivery. Today, right now, is it possible for you to get mail without the Postal Service delivering it to you? Think about it. What other ways can you get mail? Off the top of my head I can think of a few: e-mail, UPS, FedEx, Airborne, and the list goes on. The Postal Service had a motto: "Neither snow, nor rain, nor heat, nor gloom of night, stays these couriers from the swift completion of their appointed rounds." (Yes, that's different from the way most of us remember it ☺). Unfortunately for the Postal Service, it takes more than a well-crafted motto to be successful. It takes vision and non-institutional thinkers. The Postal Service had a belief that what they were doing would work and would always work for everybody, and that there was no need to change and become forward thinkers.

I agree with my young nephew that we all have what we need inside of us to be successful, but we must *use* those resources to *continue* to be successful. The Postal Service overlooked the fact that just delivering the mail would not be sufficient. What the Postal Service didn't have in their vision was excellent customer service. It doesn't matter if you're a big corporation or an individual, you need excellent customer service to succeed. The Postal Service never considered people driving by to Mailboxes, etc. (now the UPS Store) to pay extra to mail their packages. Today the Postal Service is playing catch up. They are beginning to incorporate the principles that they needed to incorporate all along.

## Driving Away from Success

Another example happened with the American automobile industry. The American automobile industry believed it knew what was best for the American consumer. The industry believed no matter what it did, Americans would buy American. It failed to have the vision and the fortitude to see what the future was going to bring. It was comfortable with the status quo. The industry continued to make bigger and bigger cars with bigger and bigger gas tanks. Soon enough, the Japanese produced a smaller, more efficient car, which used less gas. The Japanese were suddenly able to take a sizeable chunk of the car market including American consumers.

They were able to do this because nobody challenged the status quo. It appears that everybody believed that just because it had always been this way in the past, the same would be true in the future. Let me be the first or second or third to tell you this is not that case. We are all perfect yet we are not flawless. We have to continue to get resources, to get information, to create new visions, so that we can truly see. In order to move out of your own way, you have to see beyond what is already there.

## Be About the Business

When we really get down to it, each of us is an organization, and you should run your life like a business. There are key processes, strategies, and techniques that companies use to be successful. As individuals we can adopt some of these strategies to help ourselves be more successful as well. No matter who you are or what you have, you cannot rest on your laurels. You need to constantly update your equipment and continue to gain new perspectives.

**How are you thinking beyond the box?  Give specific examples**

_____

_____

_____

_____

_____

_____

_____

_____

**How does thinking beyond the box help you?**

_____

_____

_____

_____

_____

_____

_____

_____

Thinking Beyond the Box

**An African Proverb**

Every morning in Africa a gazelle gets up,
It knows it must run faster than the fastest lion or it will
be killed.
Every morning a lion wakes up.
It knows it must out run the slowest gazelle or it will
starve.

It doesn't matter whether
you are a lion or a gazelle –
when the sun comes up,
you'd better be running.

# -10-
# 15 Minutes of Fame

Have you ever thought about your 15 minutes of fame? Think about them now – think about what those 15 minutes mean to you.    Some of us might think of ourselves appearing in a commercial or a movie. Others of us might not know what we'd do with our 15 minutes of fame.    This lesson is about you *creating* your 15 minutes of fame every day. Each of us is a celebrity and that simply means we deserve to be celebrated.    Sometimes we are so bombarded with various events, people, and massive things to do lists, we don't take time out for self.    We have to learn to take time for the most important person in our lives.

I attended a seminar recently, and at the beginning of the seminar, the speaker said "I want to introduce you to a fantastic individual. A powerful, creative individual who sets goals and reaches them."  It was interesting to watch everyone look around the room in wonder. "Who is this person?" we all thought.  Many people had even decided who they thought the person was.  He didn't keep us in suspense too long though. Interestingly, the person to whom he was referring was the person sitting in our own seat.  I say that to you today.  The person reading this book is a fantastic individual who achieves goals. What I'm encouraging through this lesson is for you to celebrate your life – renew your mind, body, and soul each day.

I often hear people say they don't have time for exercise or time for themselves. They don't have time for self-renewal. Well, I am requesting you take 15 minutes each day and let that be your 15 minutes of fame. During this time you should only focus on you. You can read passages from motivational books, you can read the Bible or another inspirational text, or you can journal. However you decide to do it, just do it. The point is to really connect with yourself.

**We Can't Live Without Oxygen**
One of the most powerful lessons I've learned came while sitting on an airplane. I had just delivered a seminar and was headed home. I was exhausted, and I was tired, hungry, and late. I plopped down in my seat and half-heartedly listened to the message from the flight attendant that I had heard hundreds of times before. So frequently had I heard the speech, this time I was actually saying it along with her. A portion of the speech went something like this: "In case of loss of cabin pressure, please apply your oxygen mask first before assisting others." When she said that, a light bulb went off in me. I began to realize that while it might be a necessary procedure in flight, it is also a necessary procedure in daily life. Get this: if you don't have oxygen for yourself, you can't help anybody. Not anybody. You can't even help your dog. It's an absolute must – take care of yourself first.

Many of my clients who are mothers often question that statement at the beginning of my seminars. They tell me they absolutely *have* to put the needs of their child/children first. I simply tell them, if they don't have oxygen, they can't give anything (not love, not food) to their child. When you start to think about what could happen on a plane – if you attempted to help someone during a crisis without having sufficient oxygen yourself – you can understand the message fairly quickly. Without oxygen you may begin to laugh hysterically, have problems seeing clearly, experience lack of coordination, begin to have mental or muscle fatigue, and so on. You would never be able to assist the person you were attempting to help.

**You Can Only Give What You Have**

Often we think we are helping other people by putting ourselves second. I submit to you today, you're not helping anyone if you're not helping yourself. It's very difficult to teach any skill you don't do well. For instance, I meet many parents who want me to improve their child's self esteem, when the parents don't exhibit high self-esteem themselves. People learn from modeling behavior. If you want success for your child, you must first *be* successful yourself. One of my mentors, Dr. Wayne Dyer, speaks about giving oranges away. Think about this. Right now, from where you are, if I asked you for 27 oranges, could you give them to me? The answer for many of us is no unless you're in an orange grove or standing in the produce section of the grocery store. You don't have them, and you cannot give away what you don't have.

I am not advocating focusing on what you don't want. I am advocating being aware of what it takes to be successful. In order for you to get what you want, you have to spend some time focusing on what you want. Use your 15 minutes of fame to cultivate the pearl inside of you. For 15 minutes a day, focus on what you desire. I'm not saying that it only has to be 15 minutes. After all, the way to eat an elephant is one bite at a time. I'm encouraging you to take the first bite. If you spend a minimum of 15 minutes daily focusing on what you want, it will become easier for your life to manifest just that.

## Magnetize Your Life

The 15 minutes can be anywhere – even in the shower in the morning. I cannot begin to tell you how many thoughts for this book came while I was in the shower. In those 15 minutes I allowed ideas and thoughts to flow through me. As I allowed those ideas to flow through me, the things I needed appeared in my environment. These things could not have appeared if I had not devoted that time. Let me explain this a little more. Thomas Leonard wrote a book called *The Portable Coach*. In it, he talks about principles of attraction and how to attract things into your life. What he spoke about in many of the 28 principles was focusing on self and taking time for self. As a matter of fact, the first principle is called "Becoming Incredibly Selfish." We are going to have to understand that the more resources we devote to ourselves, the more we have for other people.

## You Can't Run on Empty

I have never seen a car that was out of gas, moving down the street. At least not without someone or something pushing it along. When the car is on E, it may go a little bit longer, but at some point, when the car is completely out of gas, it stops. If you spend time refueling your mind, your body, your spirit daily, you will not run out of gas. Think about it. As you operate on E, everything and every person you come in contact with can be a challenge. You think you're doing your child, your mate, your boss, your colleague, a favor by working on E, but let's be honest…you can't give what you don't have. The only way for you to acquire what you don't have is to spend time each day learning and exploring and focusing on you.

Use your 15 minutes of fame to cultivate the fruits within you. You are your greatest asset.

**Focusing Wisely**
Your 15 minutes of fame, celebrating your life and focusing on what it is you want, gives you the opportunity to see positive things each day you might not have been able to see. Many of us are used to focusing on what we don't have. I'm suggesting that you make a conscious choice to change your mind, thoughts, feelings, attitudes, and manifest more of what you do want. If you spend your 15 minutes focusing on what you don't want, you will get more of that. If you spend it focusing on what you do want, I guarantee you (you can call me if you don't), you will get more of that. What are those childhood dreams you are afraid to tell anyone? What would you do today if you became a millionaire? We have to learn to use our personal

energy to help us manifest and grow more of what we want.

**Activate Your Activating System**

As you focus on what you want, your reticular activating system will get it for you. As you focus on what you *don't* want, your reticular activating system will get *that* for you. Some of you might be saying, "What in the world, reticular what?" Let me explain. When you're driving down the street and you keep spotting the car you want, the system that keeps showing it to you is your reticular activating system. This is a part of your unconscious mind and its goal is to bring you what you want. Whatever your desire is, it puts it in your mind, so every time it's in your environment, you will notice it. Ironically, your unconscious mind will also help you see negative things if that's how you choose to focus your energy. Remember, the goal of your reticular activating system is to keep you happy, so if bringing negativity is what it thinks makes you happy, that's what you'll get.

Train your mind to bring you positive things. Train your mind to bring you what you want. Use your 15 minutes of fame as an armor. That 15 minutes, when used correctly, is going to protect your thoughts. Don't forget the remaining 23 hours and 45 minutes of the day. After all, every 60 seconds you still have to make a choice… I'm requesting that you always choose to be positive and that you take control of your emotions.

**Choose Happiness**

In every situation that happens, you have the opportunity to select positive things from the 2 million bits of information per second that are presented to you. It doesn't matter what has happened. So many people say, "but you don't know my story." I don't have to know your story to know that there is a more powerful angle from which to view that story.

Some of you are thinking I have claimed that nothing bad is ever going to happen to you. Actually, that's not what I'm saying. I'm saying no matter what happens, there is a way for you to view it that empowers you. Use your 15 minutes to charge your batteries, renew yourself so you can give those 27 oranges, that love, those ideas, and whatever else it is you desire to give to those you come in contact with. The Energizer Bunny may seem to keep going and going and going, but for us to be like that bunny, we must recharge!

Recently, I watched The Matrix. As I watched it, I thought about what it would mean for us to have the option of a red pill vs. a blue pill on a daily basis. When you take the red pill, you use your 15 minutes and learn to focus on what you want and manifest what you want. If you take the blue pill you continue having your life exactly as it is today.

It's your life. What pill will you take?

## How will you spend your 15 minutes of fame?

_____

_____

_____

_____

_____

_____

_____

_____

## Clearly explain your 15 minutes of fame will look like, feel like or sound like:

_____

_____

_____

_____

_____

_____

_____

_____

## What are your goals for your first session?

_____

_____

_____

_____

_____

_____

_____

# What benefits will you get from these self sessions?

_____

_____

_____

_____

_____

_____

_____

_____

_____

_____

_____

_____

_____

_____

_____

_____

_____

_____

_____

_____

_____

_____

_____

**The Value of Time**
**Author Unknown**

Imagine there is a bank that credits your account each
morning with $86,400.

It carries over no balance from day to day.

Every evening deletes whatever part of the balance
you failed to use during the day.

What would you do? Draw out every cent, of course!

Each of us has such a bank. Its name is TIME.

Every morning, it credits you with 86,400 seconds.

Every night it writes off, as lost, whatever of this you
have failed to invest to good purpose.

It carries over no balance.

It allows no overdraft.

Each day it opens a new account for you.

Each night it burns the remains of the day.

If you fail to use the day's deposits, the loss is yours.

There is no going back. There is no drawing against
the "tomorrow".

You must live in the present on today's deposits.

Invest it so as to get from it the utmost in health,
happiness and success!

The clock is running. Make the most of today.

To realize the value of ONE YEAR, ask a student who
failed a grade.

To realize the value of ONE MONTH, ask a mother
who gave birth to a pre-mature baby.

To realize the value of ONE WEEK, ask the editor of a weekly newspaper.

To realize the value of ONE DAY, ask a daily wage laborer with kids to feed.

To realize the value of ONE HOUR, ask the lovers who are waiting to meet.

To realize the value of ONE MINUTE, ask a person who missed the train.

To realize the value of ONE SECOND, ask a person who just avoided an accident.

To realize the value of ONE MILLI-SECOND, ask the person who won a silver medal in the Olympics.

Treasure every moment that you have! And treasure it more because you shared it with someone special, special enough to spend your time.

And remember that time waits for no one.

Yesterday is history.

Tomorrow is a mystery.

Today is a gift.

That's why it's called the present!

-11-
# Your Personal Board of Directors

Oprah Winfrey once said, "Everyone wants to ride with you in the limo, but what you need is someone who will take the bus with you when the limo breaks down." When I first heard that statement, it tickled me, yet over time I began to appreciate the truth in that statement. Our friends are our support system. They are there for us through our victories and our challenges, and we appreciate them for all of their special and unique qualities. Friends are people we can depend on and trust. They offer assistance, even when we don't realize it.

Building on this understanding, I'd like to introduce you to a life-changing concept: your personal Board of Directors. Like your friends, your Board of Directors is your support system. This support system isn't there to echo or agree with everything you say, or think, or do. I often tell people, if I wanted someone to agree with me all the time I would only talk to myself. As an aside, I do talk to myself often, and yes I believe that is a good thing. However, when it's time for me to make decisions in life, I broaden my audience, and look to my personal board of directors.

Let's talk a little bit about a Board of Directors. The role of a Board of Directors is to ensure the success of an organization or company. In our case, the Board is there to ensure your success. Your goal is to appoint a minimum of five people on your Board. The individuals on your Board should have a wide range of skills and behaviors that can serve as a framework for success. To be clear, what you're actually looking for are skills and behaviors you can model. What does this mean?

How many of you can remember seeing a Sean John or Vera Wang model on the runway and immediately straightening up your posture? What about being in a meeting with a person you admired or respected? You watched him or her give a brilliant presentation and magically you started to feel like that person later when it was your turn to present. You actually noticed your posture, your voice, your mannerisms, were very similar to the person you admired. This is modeling. There is a song that says "anything you can do, I can do better." Modeling makes those words possible. If there are characteristics, traits, or behaviors you like in other people, you can use those qualities or skills whenever you want them.

**Lessons from Wonder Woman**
The concept of modeling is not new to us. In his book *The People Puzzle*, Dr. Morris Massey talks about how we develop our values. He talks about a three-step process. From age 0 to 7, our values come primarily from our family, and we get those values at the unconscious level. We have no idea what we're

learning, or even that we're learning. You can almost think of yourself as a sponge soaking up values from your family.

From age 8 to 14 is the modeling stage of development. In this stage, we actually learn unconsciously *and* consciously through the process of modeling. Think back to trying on your mother's dress, or your father's shoes. As you put them on, you more than likely behaved like your mother or your father – acting out your perception of them. Essentially what you were doing was modeling their behaviors. Dr. Massey made a powerful statement in this book: he said who you modeled at 10 is who you are today.

When I first read the statement, I thought about all the influences in my life. Certainly my parents had a huge impact on me. And although I am my mother's only child, my sister and my first cousin also played a big role. As I examined this statement more deeply, I really came to realize that the person I actually modeled at 10 was Wonder Woman. You can believe that Wonder Woman is on my Board of Directors. There are several reasons why I modeled Wonder Woman. The first reason is because she was powerful. Wonder Woman was always able to handle any challenge before her. In addition, her alter ego, Diana, was brilliant. As a child growing up in the early 70s, there were not many female figures who were powerful, smart, and sexy, too. Wonder Woman had it all. She definitely made my Board of Directors.

## Modeling in Later Life

From 14 to 21 we learn through socialization. During this time, we learn consciously and unconsciously, and broaden our scope to people outside of our family and television. We begin to learn values from the outside. Dr. William James added to this. He says from 21 to 35 we develop our business persona. We are looking to people in our work environment to model our success after.

Because these stages exist, and because a lot of what we have learned has been unconscious, many of us are not able to take full advantage of the people who were influential at each stage of our lives. The concept of a personal Board of Directors is to help us create a system similar to the process that we went through in our earlier years. Our personal Board of Directors will enable us to recognize successful traits in other people and leverage those traits to make ourselves more successful. In business, companies get benchmarks and best practices to understand what the competition is doing, and to see what has been done in the area. They do this so their product will be superior, utilizing the positive assets of previously designed products. As we run our lives like a corporation, we as human beings need to employ this same tactic.

## Forming Your Board

When identifying individuals for your board of directors, the first step is to find a model of real excellence in a specific area. The second step is to understand his or her beliefs, values, and thought processes, and be aware of his or her nonverbal behaviors and overall demeanor. The third thing is to install the desired behaviors, processes, demeanor, etc. in yourself.

Every person on your board doesn't have to be someone you know personally. You should expect to perform research to truly understand the qualities and characteristics of success each possesses. Keep in mind you can learn a lot from people in power by reading their autobiographies.

You really want to understand how each person on your Board acts in given situations, and what steps each person took to achieve success in a given arena. You want to use his or her success strategies as a roadmap for your own success. This doesn't mean you'll do exactly what he or she did. It *will* mean that you can pick up the competencies and skills he or she used, and establish those behaviors in your daily life.

When identifying members for your board, remember to look for a minimum of five people. What follows is a suggested list of Board members. Do not feel limited by this list! This is a menu I've created as a starting point, but remember, you can order whatever you want!

### The President
One person on your Board can be someone holding your dream job. He or she could be in the position you're most interested in attaining. If your dream job is to be the president of the United States, then Bill Clinton (or Ronald Reagan, etc.) should be number one on your Board of Directors.

## Model of Success

Another person on your board can be someone who is successful in any area of importance to you. This can be motherhood, networking, or performance, web design, painting, or swimming, etc. The key to remember here is the person has to be successful by *your* definition of success. Pay attention to his or her attitude, behavior, language patterns, and movement. You really want to watch him or her when he or she walks into rooms and notice how people respond.

## Model of Strengths

A third person could be someone with skills that are complementary to yours. In other words, he or she could have skills you know you don't have. Spend time understanding your strengths and understanding the other individual's strengths. Then decide if you going to keep the person in your life or learn the skill set yourself. There are advantages to both. What Steven Covey says is we see the world not as it is, but as who we are. Having this third person can help you see things in a different way. This person can prevent you from being blind-sighted because of your undeveloped skills in a particular area. You may decide, however, to learn the skills in question and then replace the Model of Strengths with someone who has a different skillset you lack.

## Model of Optimism

Everybody needs a little optimism in his or her life! An optimist can enable you to learn how to frame your life challenges in a light that will be empowering to you.

There's a difference between an optimist and a sugar coater. Sugar coaters ignore the truth for a sweeter version of reality. My advice to you is to stay away from sugar coaters. According to Seligman, optimism is really about how you see things. Your optimist should be truthful, yet encouraging. You don't want to be around a person who isn't willing to tell you the truth, even when the truth is painful. When challenges appear, we want get the lesson from those obstacles, and as Tad James says, we want the lesson to be future based, positive, and related to self. Your optimist will help you understand these lessons.

## Model of Spirituality

Consider including a model for spirituality. This person can bring a spiritual perspective to the situations that will occur in your life. My advice to you is to pick someone who is more spiritual than religious, because many religions in the West are built on a foundation of guilt. There is nothing empowering about feeling guilty. Add a person to your Board of Directors who can assist you in learning life's spiritual lessons. Be mindful, this person should walk the walk, not just talk the talk.

## Modeling to Move

Modeling can help you move out of your own way. When you model, you are recognizing and appreciating successful characteristics in others. Remember, you are resourceful and you come from abundance, not lack. Use those resources inside of yourself and surround yourself with the support you need to continue to grow. As you think about history, realize whatever success people had in the past is available to you today. Just be willing to do a little exploring and see how your shero or hero made it. Take those skills for yourself so that you can make it too! You have the opportunity to be as victorious as any person that has ever existed.

## List your Board of Directors. What skill-set is each member bringing to your Board?

1. _____

2. _____

3. _____

4. _____

5. _____

## How will the Board benefit you?

_____
_____
_____
_____

## How will you benefit the Board?

_____
_____
_____
_____

# What other members would you like to add to your Board? Why?

_____

_____

_____

_____

_____

_____

_____

_____

_____

_____

_____

_____

_____

_____

_____

_____

_____

_____

_____

**Are You a Reason, a Season, or a Lifetime?**
**Author Unknown**

Pay attention to what you read. After you read this, you will know the reason it was sent to you! People come into your life for a reason, a season or a lifetime. When you figure out which one it is, you will know what to do for each person.

When someone is in your life for a REASON. . . It is usually to meet a need you have expressed. They have come to assist you through a difficulty, to provide you with guidance and support, to aid you physically, emotionally, or spiritually. They may seem like a godsend, and they are! They are there for the reason you need them to be. Then, without any wrongdoing on your part, or at an inconvenient time, this person will say or do something to bring the relationship to an end. Sometimes they die. Sometimes they walk away. Sometimes they act up and force you to take a stand. What we must realize is that our need has been met, our desire fulfilled, their work is done. The prayer you sent up has been answered. And now it is time to move on.

Then people come into your life for a SEASON. Because your turn has come to share, grow, or learn. They bring you an experience of peace, or make you laugh. They may teach you something you have never done. They usually give you an unbelievable amount of joy. Believe it! It is real! But, only for a season.

LIFETIME relationships teach you lifetime lessons: things you must build upon in order to have a solid emotional foundation. Your job is to accept the lesson, love the person, and put what you have learned to use in all other relationships and areas of your life. It is said that love is blind but friendship is clairvoyant.

# -12-
# How To Eat an Elephant

Question:    How do you eat an elephant?

Answer:    One bite at a time.

Recently, one of my friends reminded me of the quote "The most difficult task to complete is the one you never start." Do you agree with that? I can say for sure that you have to start a task if you plan to complete anything. You have to do something. I repeat – you have to *do something*. Don't wait! Procrastination is one of our biggest blockers from success. We like to say, "I'll do that tomorrow, I'll do that when I'm married, I'll do that when I have a baby, I'll do that later." The list goes on and on and on, and later never comes. Meanwhile, back at the ranch, what we really want to do, or what we *say* we really want to do, absolutely is not being done.

## Life is an Elephant

I have enjoyed writing this book because, for me, telling my story is a way for me to touch the lives of many people. The book, *Move Out of Your Own Way*, is a compilation of my life lessons. I don't believe there's anything magical or miraculous about me or my story, but what I do believe is that there's something magical and miraculous when you spread love to millions of people and that's what these stories are about.

This particular lesson about eating an elephant is so important because life is a big, or can be a humongous, colossal, gigantic, enormous elephant for many of us. You might wake up in the morning thinking about all your life's challenges, such as how am I going to do this? How I am going to do that? How am I going to pay this bill? How am I going to pick up Suzy from day care? How am I going to get a job? Everyday you might be overwhelmed with all of the "how am I going to do things lists" and it becomes difficult to do anything.

**Outrageous Notions**
One of my colleagues believes fervently the proverb of eating an elephant one bite at a time. Let's be real. If you wanted to eat an elephant right now, would you be able to just walk up and put the entire elephant in your mouth? I know that might sound crazy, but I have to say these things because I want you to hear and feel where I am coming from. As you think about how outrageous that concept might be, you can start to think about how outrageous it might be on a daily basis for you to try to put your own elephant in your mouth everyday. We try, unsuccessfully to eat whole elephants *everyday*.

So I ask you, how do you eat an elephant? Rather than walking up to the elephant and trying to shove it in our mouth, break it down into bite-sized chunks. Let us make the elephant something we can manage, something we can handle. Figure out the pieces of whatever it is that is challenging you. Decide what it is you can handle at this particular point in your life.

## First Things First

Before we get into that, let us figure out what is it you want. Take some time right now and jot down what it is you want. I know that sounds like a cliché, but really, what is it? What do you really, truly want? There are all types of books, cassettes, etc. out there on that, but that is the first question that you absolutely need to ask yourself. What is it that you actually want?

## Get the Picture

After you figure out what is it that you want, ask yourself what is it going to take to get that? Just think about it, what is it going to take? Then start to think about the benefits. If you make a million dollars tomorrow, what will happen? You'll pay off some bills? Buy some things for your loved ones? What will that million dollars get for you? Really, get into the physiology or the feeling. There's a great book called *Excuse Me, Your Life is Waiting*, and the author of that book spends a lot of time describing how to get into the feeling of what it is that you want. As you start to feel what it is you want, then you start to create the energy that you need to actually start getting it done. So, what will "it" get for you?

Go ahead and imagine yourself with "it." What do you see? If it's a trip to Cancun, go ahead and imagine yourself out there on the beach. Picture yourself with the beautiful sand around you. See yourself parasailing. Visualize yourself snorkeling. Envision yourself having a massage on the ocean. Fantasize about doing whatever it is that you want to do. Really see yourself in the picture. Now, step out of the picture. Step out of the picture and see the picture without you in it. Those steps will help you bite the elephant. Once you get into the picture, you have begun to move your spirit in that direction. When you then remove yourself, your mind suddenly has the need to complete the picture – with you in it! You set in motion the energy needed to get the task done.

## Bite-sized pieces – a chunk at a time

You can chunk your life into manageable pieces. The concept of chunking is not new. Even the people that created the social security number know that it would be hard to bite a whole elephant at one time. It is not by accident that your social security number is chunked 222-22-2222. Those are chunks. Your social security number is presented that way so that you can easily identify it. Think about your phone number 867-5309. The phone company knows about chunking too. You have an area code, an exchange, and the last part of the number. You learn it and recite it with the pauses. That is chunking information. So why is it that we think that we need to do everything at one moment? It is all about chunking. It is all about laying out the map, looking at the vision, and seeing what has to be done now. Go ahead and create a project plan for yourself. Treat your life as if you were running a business. Create a project plan, step by step, systematically.

## Take out the Trash

Tony Robbins actually talks about a wastebasket theory that I love. His wastebasket theory is a great one to help people move out of their own way one step at a time. This theory encourages you to do a project as if it were going in the trashcan. For example, imagine you wanted to write a book. You tell yourself that you are going to write X amount of lines for a certain period of time, but you do not put the pressure on yourself to make those lines perfect. You can intend to throw those lines away when you're done, your only goal being to complete them in the first place. What happens many times is we start to think about making our project perfect, and we realize perfection is so difficult to attain that we do nothing. We do absolutely nothing. We want the perfect shoes and workout outfit, meanwhile we never start to exercise. We want the perfect name for our screenplay, so we don't start writing it. Nothing gets done. Don't strive for perfection…strive for completion. Just get started.

## Take Things Slowly

The most difficult task to complete is the one you never start. You absolutely have to start a task in order to complete it. I would not ask you today to come with me and run a marathon. If I did, you would probably think I was a little bit off my rocker. The truth of the matter is some of us wake up in the morning with these visions that we can run a marathon, that day, without the training, without any of the exercise, without any of the preparation that goes into running a marathon. It takes time and preparation to do things.

- Be gentle with yourself.
- Be loving and allow yourself the opportunity to do what it is that you need to do.
- Focus on the priority, the immediate things that need to be done.

- Then think about the long-term things that need to be done and create a step-by-step process for that.

If you are running the marathon next year, there is no need to be concerned with how many miles you are going to run today. What you need to be concerned about is taking the first step, which may be getting on the treadmill today, for however long you can stay on the treadmill (even if it's only one or two minutes). Yes, it is wonderful to have the vision, to see yourself running the marathon. Visualize yourself running the marathon, but do not allow your anxiety or your fear from that to rule you. All you need to do today is begin. If you just got up today and walked around briskly for 5 minutes, at least you started something!

**Use Good Table Manners**
You are learning the concept of eating the elephant one bite at a time. Take bite-sized chunks. I have never seen a person (and you might have because there are shows out there like Ripley's Believe it or Not, and there is the Guinness Book of World Records, so there are many different things possible out there), but I personally have never seen a person swallow a whole steak. Generally a person will cut a piece of steak and put that that piece in his or her mouth and begin to chew. Those same lessons that we use with food, we can use with our life. So, take your time. Have faith in the process and understand that it is ok for you to take one step at a time.

## Babies Can Do It, So Can You

Consider the first time that you probably ever walked in your life. I am a psychologist and I do not know many children who ran the same day they took their first step. Meditate on that. Why is it that we feel that we have to take on so many things at one time? Be gentle with yourself.

If cleaning your room is a difficult task for you, then guess what? Get a timer, set it for 30 minutes and clean a portion of it. Okay? Do not think about the entire room... think about a section of it. Walk in and say, "My goal for now is to clean this portion," or "Let me clean this drawer." Do not try to clean all 12 drawers in your dresser or chest of drawers. Focus on one at a time. Now, what's interesting is that once you start, you have achieved a win! Later, after several starts, the adrenaline begins to flow, and you're able to clean all the drawers, to run the marathon, to do all of those things, because you have had a few checks in the "Win" column.

The key is to get a few successes under your belt and develop the discipline. Do what it is you said you are going to do, but do it one step at a time. One bite at a time.

## Get it Done

As I finish this book, I am being challenged on every chapter I am writing. I am practicing what I preach. I am not going to say it's easy. Things come up when you start to put things out to the universe. I told as many people as I knew when the book was going to be done, so I would have to take a bite-sized chunk every week and get it done. *Get it done.* It has been a challenge to carve out the time to do this project. What I had to do for myself is to say, "The elephant is the book, but you don't have to do the entire book in one night. Nobody is expecting that. All you have to do is one chapter at a time. And really, just one passage or thought at a time."

I first started this project, over two years ago, and I'll be very honest with you, I've gotten done more in the last two months than I have in the past two years. The reason why is because I have learned to take small chunks. In the beginning, I was getting the book title, the cover, trying to figure out the chapters, doing all of these things at one time; meanwhile back at the ranch, the book was not being completed because I was getting overwhelmed. So I said, "Here's my timetable and here is what I can do. These are thoughts for my chapters."

Once I did that, adrenaline began flowing. More resources came from the universe. My editor came along and helped me to create a vision of how the book could come out of me to you, which alone I would have never ever been able to create. One of my assistants came forward and basically said what can I do? I realized all I needed to do was do my little piece.

**Let "One Day" Start Today**
I am inviting you to figure out the project you'd like to complete or the vision you have for your life. It does not have to be a book, but what do you want? You

know your resources and you also know that by not sharing them with the universe we are not benefiting from them right now. What is it that you need to get done, or what is it that you are allowing to overwhelm you? Think about it, write it down. Develop a *simple* action plan. Get a process. Figure out today, right now, how you can get *one* thing done, one day at a time.

Dr. Benjamin E. Mays used to say:

> The tragedy of life is often not in our failure but rather in our complacency, not in doing too much, but rather in doing too little, not in our living above our ability but rather in our living below our capacities.

He also had another quote I'd like to share with you:

> It must be born in mind that the tragedy of life doesn't lie in not reaching your goal, the tragedy lies in having no goal to reach. It is not a calamity to die with dreams unfulfilled, but it is a calamity not to dream. It is not a disaster to be unable to capture your idea, but it is a disaster to have no idea to capture. It is not a disgrace not to reach the stars, but it is a disgrace to have no stars to reach for. Not failure, but low aim is sin.

## Move Minute by Minute

Stop blocking yourself. Move out of our own way. Create a plan that will allow you to take things one day at a time. I mean, really, take it one day at a time. With that plan, do the best you have can what you have. That is all that I am asking. That is all anyone can ask. Be the best you that you can be. Do not get overwhelmed. Just take one step at a time. There is a final quote Mays used often, though the original author is unknown. It is sometimes referred to as God's Minute:

I have only just a minute.
Only 60 seconds in it.
Forced upon me, can't refuse it.
Did not seek it, did not choose it, but it's up to me to use it.
I must suffer if I lose it; give account if I abuse it.
Just a tiny little minute, but eternity is in it.

## From Impossible to Possible

As you think about each moment of your day, I am asking you to make them bite-sized portions. I know you might want to eat everything on the buffet, but it is pretty hard to do it at one time. It is pretty difficult to do it at one sitting. Take your time. Eat the elephant one bite at a time and create success for yourself. Figure out what you can do and do that.

Saint Frances of Assisi encouraged: "Start by doing what's necessary, then do what's possible and suddenly you are doing the impossible." And I know that you can do the impossible because you wouldn't be reading this book if you didn't know how many resources are available to you, how powerful you are, and what you have to offer. People do not read books like this who are not great people. The people who read books like this are already great, and they are finding ways they can become greater. That is really what Move Out of Your Own Way is about, you being better. The only person you have to compete with is yourself.

Start by doing what is necessary, then do what's possible and suddenly, suddenly, suddenly, you will be doing the impossible! If you are not, e-mail me, call me and let me know, because I know you will accomplish all of your dreams. You're going to get what you want because you're going to focus on it. You are going to do what is necessary, you are going to do what is possible and all of a sudden you are going to wake up and you are going to be doing the impossible.

**Congratulations!**

## What is your elephant?

_____

_____

_____

_____

_____

_____

_____

_____

## What bite-sized pieces will you chunk your elephant into?

Step One:

_____

Step Two:

_____

Step Three:

_____

Step Four:

_____

Step Five

_____

Step Six:

_____

Step Seven:

_____

Step Eight:
_____

Step Nine:
_____

Step Ten:
_____

**In what step will you use the wastebasket theory?**
_____
_____
_____

**What date will you start?**
_____

**What is your timeline?**_____

**Celebrate after each step!**

**List your successes:**
_____
_____
_____
_____
_____
_____
_____
_____

How to Eat an Elephant

**Just For Today**
**Author Unknown**

Just for today I will live through the next 12 hours and not tackle my whole life's problems at once.

Just for today I will improve my mind. I will learn something useful. I will read something that requires effort, thought, and concentration.

Just for today I will be agreeable, I will look my best, speak in a well-modulated voice, be courteous and considerate.

Just for today I will not find fault with friend, relative, or colleague. I will not try to change or improve anyone but myself.

Just for today I will have a program. I might not follow it exactly, but I will have it. I will save myself from two enemies-hurry and indecision.

Just for today I will exercise my character in three ways. I will so a good turn and keep it a secret. If anyone finds out, it won't count.

Just for today I will do two things I don't want to do, just for exercise.


Just for today I will be unafraid. Especially will I be unafraid to enjoy what is beautiful and believe that as I give to the world, the world will give to me.

# Afterword

Some of the most important lessons in life come at times when we aren't looking. I have heard them referred to as "teachable moments." In that moment, you take what is presented to you and make the most of it. You learn from it. You grow from it. In these moments your entire meaning or existence can actually start to make sense. The synapses in your brain actually light up and new connections are created in a way that you never even knew possible.

When you look back, you begin to try to figure out "how" you were finally able to connect the dots. To be honest, the only thing that comes clear about how you were able to evolve or grow is that you had little if any to do with it. It is times like these that we strive to make perfect sense of things that aren't always designed to have perfect logic attached to them. You immediately realize that the lesson came from a higher source in the universe and you were only the instrument used to edify or communicate the lessons.

Once we step back and realize this point we can start on the journey of the "selves": self-movement, self awareness, self-less ness, self discovery, and self love. On this path we realize that our trials and triumphs are actually not individual struggles, but opportunities for God (or any supreme being) to carry us through. Let me say here that whatever we call God should not be used to separate humankind. God should be used to unite us. God is good all the time! As I write to you today, I am not Catholic, but I have been praying to St.

Anthony per Mama Das' request to help me find opportunities. I don't have to be Catholic to respect and treasure their beliefs.

One key message that has been a teachable moment in my life was the realization that diversity of thought applies to religion. In order for me to reach my epiphany and get a deeper connection with God, I actually had to be open to different forms of communication and communion with God. On my journey of self-recovery, I actually learned more about "self" as I learned more about God's plan for me in the universe. It was like one day my soul just opened up and God started pouring consciousness, love, forgiveness, empathy, wisdom, and abundance into me.

Once God started pouring these items into my soul, I started to "see' things, people and life in a different light. Different messages of confirmation were sent directly to my spirit. I'll share one with you now. At that time I would have called it a coincidence. (Now that I've started on the path I know that there are no "coincidences" every thing in your life is EXACTLY as it should be). At that time, I was on the phone with Tonjua and she said, "My aunt would say this is your season." One of the things about me is I don't typically accept things at face value. (I enjoy being a critical thinker). I said, "What do you mean it is my season?" She replied, "Your season" and left the rest for me to discover own my own. Well within a period of days, three other people who are *seemingly* not connected to Tonjua (because we truly are all connected and related), said the same thing. "It is your season." Well when they all said it was my season I began to do what many spiritual people do – I got frightened. I started to think that God really might have a plan for my life that I didn't know anything about. WOW! What a concept. God has a plan for my life that I am not aware of.

All the time the "It's your season" comments were coming, I was saying the Prayer of Jabez every morning and any time through the day that I thought about it. I was feeding my soul with Dr. Norman Vincent Peale, Dr. Wayne Dyer, Dr. Dennis Kimbro, and Zig Ziglar just to name a few, and each of these sources began to help me start a plan that would lead me to manifesting my destiny and purpose through God.

I have always had an intimate relationship with positive thinking. As long as I can remember I have listened to positive thinking tapes. When I was young my mom used to play the tapes while she was sleeping. Eventually, I started doing the same. I was probably the only 5th grader quoting Dr. Norman Vincent Peale. Interestingly, I have always known that because of those experiences, one day I would be called to share the positive thinking with others. I don't share because I think I am better than you or I know more than you, I share because I enjoy it. I love the messages and key points that I have learned in my life. Sharing these messages reminds me of a song my late Aunt Em used to sing to me, "If I can help somebody along the way then my living will not be in vain."

God has been preparing me to share this message for along time. I began listening to Dr. Peale at age 5 was so that I could honestly say that I have over 25 years experience in the area of positive thinking and self work. The steps of a good woman are ordered and I thank God that my steps are! Please enjoy the lessons. They were truly a labor of love and herein may you have found the fruits of my labor.

Create a powerful day!

Dr. Cherry A. Collier

# About the Author

Dr. Cherry is the Chief Collaboration Officer and Master Certified Coach of Personality Matters, Inc. She empowers individuals and organizations to recognize and value their human potential leading to increased satisfaction and collaboration at home, at work, and in the community.

She received her M.S. and Ph.D. in Social Psychology from the University of Georgia. She is a college professor, executive consultant, and facilitator of change. Master Certified Coach (ICF and ABNLP) and certified in TTI assessment tools, HBDI, DISC, CPI and True Colors. She thinks greatness is in you and is so happy you want to join the MOVEment!!

Please write us and tell us about your experience with the book!
askdrcherry@gmail.com

Or call 404.287.0619
We want to know that you moved out of your own way!

Also ask us how you can make money selling the book through our affiliate program.

# Resources

*A Course in Miracles Published by Foundation For Inner Peace.*
*P.O. Box 598 Mill Valley, CA 94942.* www.acim.org

A Return To Love: Reflections on the Principles of A Course in
Miracles By: Marianne Williamson

*Attitude is Everything* by Keith Harrell. HarpersCollins
Publishers, Inc. 10 East 53rd Street, New York, NY 10022.

*A Woman's Path to Wholeness* by Carolyn Porter. Empower
Productions, 205 Ridgepoint Court, Woodstock, GA 30188.

*An Attitude of Gratitude* by Keith D. Harrell. Hay House, Inc.,
P.O. Box 5100, Carlsbad, CA 92018-5100.

*Developing the Leader Within You* by John C. Maxwell. Thomas
Nelson Publishers, Nashville, TN.

*Don't Sweat the Small Stuff and it's all small stuff* by Richard
Carlson, Ph.D. Hyperion, 77 West 66th Street, New York, NY
10023-6298.

Doug Stevenson Unlimited, 2104 Sussex Lane, Colorado
Springs, CO 80909. www.dougstevenson.com.

*Emotional Intelligence Video* with Daniel Goleman. PBS Home
Video, Washington, D.C.

*Empowering Yourself* by Harvey J. Coleman. Kendall/Hunt
Publishing Company, 4050 Westmark Drive, Dubuque, Iowa
52002.

*Expect A Miracle-Make Miracles Happen* by Norman Vincent
Peale, taken from Guideposts Magazine. Guideposts Associates,
Inc., Carmel, New York 10512.

Excuse Me Your Life is Waiting: The Astonishing Power of Feelings by Lynn Grabhorn

*Finding Flow by Mihaly Csikszentmihalyi.* Basic Books, HarpersCollins Publishers, Inc. 10 East 53rd Street, New York, NY 10022.

*Fish!* by Stephen C. Lundin, Ph.D., Harry Paul and John Christensen. Hyperion, 77 West 66th Street, New York, NY 10023-6298.

Get the Edge by Anthony Robbins.

*Great Quotes from Zig Ziglar.* Career Press, 3 Tice Road, P.O. Box 687, Franklin Lakes, NJ 07417.

*Guard Your Gates!* by Dale Carnegie Bronner. Carnegie Books, 2435 Ben Hill Road, East Point, GA 30344.

*Hypnosis: A Comprehensive Guide* by Tad James, Ph.D., Crown House Publishing.

*In the Meantime* by Iyanla Vanzant. Simon & Schuster, Rockafeller Center, 1230 Avenue of the Americas, New York, NY 10020.

*Jonathan Livingston Seagull.* 5555 Melrose Avenue, Hollywood, CA 90038.

*Learned Optimism* featuring the Author, Martin E.P. Seligman, Ph.D., Simon and Schuster Audio. 1230 Avenue of the Americas, New York, NY 10020.

*Legacy of the Heart* by Wayne Muller. Fireside, Rockafeller Center, 1230 Avenue of the Americas, New York, NY 10020.

*Manifest your Destiny* by Dr. Wayne W. Dyer. HaperCollins Publishers, 10 East 53rd Street, New York, NY 10022.

*Man's Search for Meaning* by Viktor E Frankl. Touchstone Books, Rockafeller Center, 1230 Avenue of the Americas, New York, NY 10020.

*Meditation for Busy People* by Dawn Groves. Barnes & Noble Books, NY.

*Now, Discover your Strengths* by Marcus Buckingham and Donald O. Clifton, Ph.D., The Free Press, 1230 Avenue of the Americas, New York, NY 10020.

*O, The Oprah Magazine.*

*One Day my Soul Just Opened up* by Iyanla Vanzant. Fireside, Rockafeller Center, 1230 Avenue of the Americas, New York, NY 10020.

*Please Understand Me* by David Keirsey and Marilyn Bates. Prometheus Nemesis Book Company, Box 2748, Del Mar, CA 92014.

*Putting the One Minute Manager to Work* by Kenneth Blanchard, Ph.D., and Robert Lorber, Ph.D., Berkley Publishing Group, 200 Madison Avenue, New York, NY 10016.

*Quantum Healing, Exploring the Frontiers of Mind/Body Medicine.* By Deepak Chopra, M.D., Bantam Books, New York.

*Rich Dad, Poor Dad* by Robert T. Kiyosaki. Time Warner Audio Books, www.twbookmark.com/audiobooks.

*Robbing the Grave of Its Greatness!* by Delatorro L. McNeal II, A Noval Idea, Inc., P.O. Box 27242, Tampa, FL 33623.

*Running with the Giants* by John C. Maxwell. Warner Books.

*Secrets of the Vine* by Bruce Wilkinson. Multnomah Publishers, Inc., P.O. Box 1720, Sisters, Oregon 97759.

*Six Weeks to Words of Power* by Wilfred Funk. Wilfred Funk, Inc.

*Success and the Self-Image* read by Zig Ziglar. Simon and Schuster Audio. 1230 Avenue of the Americas, New York, NY 10020.

*Success One Day at a Time* by John C. Maxwell. Maxwell Motivation, Norcross, GA 30092.

*Spiritual Insights into the Genius of Leonardo da Vinci* a dialog between Michael J. Gelb and Deepak Chopra, M.D., Hay House Audio.

*10 Secrets For Success And Inner Peace by Dr. Wayne Dyer. Hay House, Inc.*

*The 7 Habits of Highly Effective People* by Stephen R. Covey. Simon and Schuster, Rockafeller Center, 1230 Avenue of the Americas, New York, NY 10020.

*The 50 Miracle Principles of A Course IN Miracles* by Kenneth Wapnick, Ph.D. Foundation for A Course In Miracles, 1275 Tennanah Lake Road, Roscoe, NY 12776-5905.

*The Artist's Way* by Julia Cameron. Penguin Putnam Inc., 375 Hudson Street, New York, NY 10014.

*The Cookie Thief* ~Author: Valerie Cox~ From A 3rd Serving of Chicken Soup for the Soul Copyright 1996 by Jack Canfield and Mark Victor.

*The Greatest Miracle in the World* by Og Mandino. Frederick Fell Publishers Inc., Compact Books, Inc., 2500 Hollywood Blvd., Suite 302, Hollywood, FL, 33020.

*The Greatest Salesman in the World* by Og Mandino. Frederick Fell Publishers, Inc., 2131 Hollywood Blvd., Suite 204, Hollywood, FL 33020.

*The Little Book of Etiquette* by Sheila M. Long. Barnes & Noble, Inc.

*The Magic of Thinking Big* by David Schwartz, Ph.D., Fireside, Rockafeller Center, 1230 Avenue of the Americas, New York, NY 10020.

*The Maxwell Leadership Bible* by John C. Maxwell. Thomas Nelson Publishers, P.O. Box 141000, Nashville, TN.

*The People Puzzle* by Morris Massey. Reston Publishing Company, Inc., Reston, VA.

*The Power of Positive Thinking by Dr. Norman Vincent Peale. Simon & Schuster Sound Ideas.*

*The Portable Coach* by Thomas J. Leonard. Scribner, 1230 Avenue of the Americas, New York, NY 10020.

*The Purpose Driven Life* by Rick Warren. Zondervan, Grand Rapids, Michigan 49530.

*The Realness of a Woman* by Carolyn Porter, D.Div. Empower Productions, 205 Ridgepoint Court, Woodstock, GA 30188.

*The Seat of the Soul* by Gary Zukav. Fireside, Rockafeller Center, 1230 Avenue of the Americas, New York, NY 10020. (and audio).

*The Tipping Point* by Malcolm Gladwell. Little, Brown and Company, Boston.

*The Wiz by* Joel Schumacher.

*The Wizard of Oz by* L. Frank Baum.

*The Worst-Case Scenario Survival Handbook: Dating and Sex* by Joshua Piven, David Borgenicht, and Jennifer Worick. Chronicle Books, 85 Second Street, San Fransisco, CA 94105.

*The Yoga Sutras of Patanjali* by Alistair Shearer. Bell Tower, New York, NY.

*There is a Spiritual Solution to Every Problem by Dr. Wayne Dyer. Hay House Audio*

*Think and Grow Rich* by Napoleon Hill. Fawcett Books, Napoleon Hill Foundation, 1440 Paddock Drive, Northbrook, IL 60062.

*Time Line Therapy and the Basis of Personality* by Tad James and Wyatt Woodsmall. Meta Publications, P.O. Box 1910, Capitola, CA 95010.

*To Change the Future, Change the Children!* by Toni E. Weaver, Ph.D. Voices Publishing, P.O. Box 13, Vandalia, OH 45377-0013.

*Running with the Giants* by John C. Maxwell. Warner Books.

*Showing our True Colors* by Mary Miscisin. True Colors, Inc. Publishing, 12395 Doherty Street, Riverside, CA 92503.

*Understanding Your Potential* by Myles Munroe. Destiny Image Publishers, Inc., P.O. Box 351 , Shippensburg, PA 17257-0351.

*What Makes the Great Great* by Dennis P. Kimbro, Ph.D. Doubleday, 1540 Broadway, New York, NY 10036.

*Who Moved My Cheese* by Spencer Johnson, M.D., G.P. Putnam's Sons. New York, NY 10014.

*Why Can't You See Me?* By Christopher J. Cokley and Aaron M. Blake. Love Life Publishing, LLC., 175 W Weicua Rd NE, Suite 211, Atlanta, GA 30342.

*Why Settle?* by Jonathan Sprinkles. Sprinkilisms, www.sprinkilisms.com.

*Wishcraft, How to get what you really Want* by Barbara Sher with Annie Gottlieb. Ballantine Books, New York.

*You Can Heal Your Life* by Louise L. Hay. Hay House Inc., P.O. Box 5100, Carlsbad, CA 92018-5100.

*101 Gems of Greatness* by Delatorro L. McNeal, II. A Noval Idea, Inc., P.O. Box 27242, Tampa, FL 33623.